The Aims, Role and Deployment of Staff in the Nursery

Philip Clift
Shirley Cleave
Marion Griffin

NFER Publishing Company

710173676-9

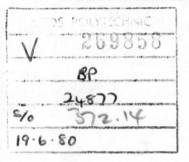
Published by the NFER Publishing Company Ltd.,
Darville House, 2 Oxford Road East,
Windsor, Berks. SL4 1DF
Registered Office: The Mere, Upton Park, Slough, Berks. SL1 2DQ.
First published 1980
© NFER
Limp Cover ISBN 0 85633 197 X

Typeset by The Yale Press, S.E.25
Printed and bound in Great Britain by
REDWOOD BURN LIMITED
Trowbridge & Esher

Distributed in the USA by Humanities Press Inc.,
Atlantic Highlands, New Jersey 07716 USA.

Contents

Acknowledgements

This project was commissioned by the Department of Education and Science (DES) following the announcement by the Government in 1972 that it intended to expand nursery education in accordance with the recommendations of the Plowden and Gittens Reports. Martin Woodhead was responsible for the research design, and was project leader until September 1977, by which time the field work had been completed. The responsibility for the initial analysis of the data, and the preparation of early drafts of the report fell mainly upon Shirley Cleave, Marion Griffin, and Wendy Fader of NFER Statistical Services. This present version was written by Philip Clift and Shirley Cleave, after consultation with and advice from staff at the DES, including Her Majesty's Inspectors, and further analyses of data by Wendy Fader. Dorothy Merritt was Project Secretary throughout. She gave invaluable support, and was responsible for typing the several drafts of the report.

The project team wish to acknowledge their gratitude for guidance and support from the DES Liaison Committee chaired by Miss Jennifer Banbury. They also wish to acknowledge the help given by staff – advisers and administrators – in the 11 local education authorities involved in the study. Most especially they wish to thank the nursery staff – 40 teachers and 40 assistants – who so willingly completed lengthy questionnaires, submitted to interviews, and, undismayed, went about their daily business apparently unaffected by the radio microphones, the stop watches and the clip-boards.

NFER
June 1979

Foreword

When in 1972 the Government announced its intention to expand educational provision for children of under five years of age, the Social Science Research Council commissioned a review[1] of current research into pre-school education. The purpose of the review was to highlight topics about which knowledge was scanty, so that research into them might subsequently be undertaken.

Of the behaviour of staff in the nursery, the reviewer suggested (page 9):

> It would therefore seem important especially for those responsible for staff training, to examine the processes going on within the school, to see whether children's achievements can be related to the minute by minute characteristics of staff behaviour, and to study the factors which affect staff behaviour. From an administrative point of view it is also important to know whether there are clear advantages to the employment of teachers rather than nursery nurses; for the College of Education it is important to know whether beliefs and attitudes about education do indeed influence the way in which staff behave.

Three research projects were set up to investigate these issues. One, a study of teacher-effectiveness,[2] tried to relate differences in observed teacher practices to differences in the behaviour of the children in their care, on the assumption that there is a causal link proceeding from the teachers. Its report is not yet available. The second set out to change teacher behaviour in the hope of producing related changes in children's achievements. Of it the senior author[3] concludes: '... altering teachers' behaviour does not necessarily result in altering children's achievements in the expected way. What is learnt often differs from what is taught.' Aside from mildly querying the use of a verb as inherently didactic in emphasis as 'taught' in connection with nursery education, this statement disappoints, but provokes little surprise or dissent.

In both of these studies an attempt was made to relate staff behaviour to that of the children in their care. In the third study, *Aims, Role and Deployment of Staff in the Nursery*, no such attempt was made. Instead, its purpose was to provide evidence of a more descriptive nature about what staff actually do, moment by moment in the nursery. It also attempted to establish whether the training and tradition of the two nursery professions, their expressed aims, and their responsibilities ascribed and perceived, influence the way they behave in the nursery. Finally it was addressed implicitly to the delicate issue of 'whether there are clear advantages to the employment of nursery teachers rather than nursery nurses.'

The report begins with a brief introduction to nursery education, and to post-Plowden nursery research. The training and tradition of the two professions which staff the nursery are then reviewed in Chapter 2. The way in which each has professional links elsewhere, the teachers with Education, the assistants with Social Services, are contrasted as being of depth and breadth respectively.

The local education authorities in which the study took place are introduced in Chapter 3, the nurseries, schools, units and classes, are described; then details of the staff – 40 teachers and 40 assistants – are given. Their training, both initial and in-service, and their prior professional experience is considered in the light of the general picture given in Chapter 2. The chapter concludes by discussing staff perceptions of the constraints under which they were working.

Chapter 4 further sets the scene for the study by portraying the range of nursery activities provided by the nurseries in the study, then moves on to the discussion of planning procedures, and concludes by reporting the attitudes of staff to nursery organization, illustrated by quotations.

Having introduced the staff in the context of their training and traditions, their aims – what they are trying to achieve – are then discussed in Chapter 5, and their role (defined as the responsibilities which are ascribed to them by their superiors, and their responsibilities as they themselves perceive them) is discussed in Chapter 6.

What is presented thus far is *contextual* information, progressing from broad generalities about the nature of nursery education, current research, and professional identity, to environmental features, personal characteristics, attitudes and beliefs. The rest of the report presents information which was obtained by direct observation.

A general task definition for all staff, teachers and assistants, is presented in Chapter 7. It derives from an aggregate of about 400 hours of intensive continuous observation. It describes staff life in the nursery in terms of: proportion of time overall spent on various tasks; frequency of changes of task; average length of episodes of the various tasks; who the tasks were done with; who initiated changes of task.

Having reviewed the observed activities of staff (teachers and assistants) collectively, their differential deployment is described in Chapter 8, and their differential use of language in Chapter 9.

Finally, the interdependent nature of the work of staff in the nursery is examined in Chapter 10, which concludes by discussing the influence of role differentiation of deployment.

The data on the basis of which this report has been prepared were obtained by the use of a variety of research instruments – interview and observation schedules, questionnaires and checklists – developed specially for the study. They are introduced as appropriate throughout the report, side-by-side with the data they yielded, and are included as Appendix A, along with instructions for their use.

Each of the 40 nurseries in the study was visited for a total of six sessions (half-days) for the collection of the various data. Observations were carried out only during the nursery sessions, not before or after, and it is therefore not possible, on the basis of direct observation, to confirm or deny that 'planning' was carried out regularly before and after sessions by staff, nor, on the basis of direct observation, is it possible to confirm or deny that it was a co-operative as distinct from individual activity.

References

1. TIZARD, B. (1974). *Early Childhood Education: A Review and Discussion of Research in Britain.* Windsor: NFER
2. CASHDAN, A. (n.d.). *Teaching Styles in Nursery Education.* An Open University research project: Faculty of Educational Studies, Walton Hall, Milton Keynes, Bucks.
3. TIZARD, B. (n.d.). *Staff and Child Behaviour in the Pre-school.*

Chapter 1

Introduction: Nursery Education and Research

Introduction: nursery education and research

In England and Wales, the nursery stage has developed later and in a more piecemeal fashion than most other stages in education. A few years ago, with the publication of The White Paper (1972),[1] it seemed about to enter a period of sustained growth, but economic events since then have to date confounded that late promise.

Traditionally the emphasis in nursery education was on children's physical and social needs.[2] More recently a different emphasis emerged, the general philosophy of which was that of 'positive discrimination': making nursery education selectively available to families considered to be socially and culturally deprived. The aim was to compensate for this early deprivation by providing an educationally enriched experience for the children, thereby enabling them to take fuller advantage of their subsequent statutory education. Objective means of identifying which children should be offered nursery places in this spirit of positive discrimination was the focus of various research projects,[3] and the concept of being 'at risk', socially and educationally, was developed, and attempts were made to give it empirical definition. Schemes for remedying the 'defects' apparently manifest in the children at risk were also developed and evaluated under varying degrees of experimental control.

On the whole results have been disappointing,[4] and it may well be that the expectation that nursery education could substantially and permanently alter the nature and prospects of certain children was misconceived, and hence at a practical level impossible to achieve. That is certainly the conclusion of a recent review of research in this area.[5]

This failure in expectations does not in any way imply that nursery education does not have value as a stage in education in its own right. It was the attempt to justify it mainly in terms of its selective application to the 'cycle of deprivation' which is seen now to have been over-optimistic.

However, it may well be that the search for viable compensatory programmes served a useful purpose in that they focused attention on to the aims of nursery education, and in particular the degree to which intellectual development might be given greater emphasis in relation to the more traditional emphasis on physical and social needs.

In fact, little objective evidence existed concerning these relative emphases, when the Plowden Report[6] recommended that there should be a considerable expansion in nursery education provision. Two studies were immediately commissioned by the Schools Council: *Pre-School Education*,[7] a two-year 'study of good practice' in nursery schools, classes and other forms of pre-school education; and *A Study of Nursery Education*,[8] which was an extension to an already existing project, *Aims of Primary Education*. In the former, visits were made to pre-school establishments and reception classes in infant schools, and interviews concerning nursery education were conducted with the adults involved. From this study emerged a list of criteria for establishments 'deemed good'. In the latter, teachers involved in nursery education were first of all asked for statements of their aims and purposes, and later asked to rate them. The report on the latter concludes (page 61) that there were 'unresolved contradictions and complexities in the field of nursery education', and it had been 'unable to establish a clear relationship between the major purposes of nursery education and the objectives by which these purposes are translated into educational practices', and that perhaps' '... the only way to show a clearer relationship between broad aim and specific intent is to show it at the level of practice in the nursery school and class'.

What both studies clearly lacked were data based on actual practices and daily activities as observed in nursery schools and classes. This is not to suggest that teachers and others claim to have aims which they then wilfully ignore or contradict in practice, but rather that the degree to which different aims are emphasized and to which apparently contradictory aims are reconciled in practice, was simply not known.

At the end of 1972 the Government announced that it intended to expand nursery education in accordance with the recommendations of the Plowden and Gittens Reports. Early in 1973, Circulars 2/73 and 39/73 were sent to local authorities giving guidance as to the scope and nature of this expansion. In principle the expansion was to be in response to parental demand, and to be made available to children from the school term after they were three until the school term after they were five, when they would be of an age to be required to attend (infant) school by law.

Expansion to meet parental demand, whilst not inherently a contradiction of the notion of 'positive discrimination' as applied to nursery education, might however be expected to occur in places where the economic means were plentiful, and where the political tactics appropriate to demand were well understood. Nursery education as a stage in its own right, rather than as a selective leveller, was implicitly endorsed. Since considerable freedom was to have been given in shaping the growing provision in response to perceived local needs and existing services, it was decided at the outset that the process should be monitored. Sums of money were allocated to this purpose by the DES, and a short term study by HMI was undertaken to determine the optimum scope and content of a suitable programme of research.

This project, *Aims, Role and Deployment of Staff in the Nursery*, was one of the first round of projects commissioned in this programme. Its focus was the work of staff in the nursery, and its principal method was structured observation.

The use of the term 'staff' is important. Unlike most other stages of education, nursery education is staffed not just by one group of professionals, but by two: nursery teachers and nursery assistants. Furthermore, whilst team teaching is being cautiously introduced in other stages of education, the presence of only one adult with a nursery class is the rare exception, the presence of three or even four (including students and parents) being relatively common. This study, of the practice of aims in the nursery, thus necessarily incorporates also the study of the interaction of professionals from different backgrounds, in relation to their ascribed and perceived responsibilities.

The Management Committee for Nursery Education Research, set up by the DES to deal with the development of the monitoring programme, initially considered that the main practical value of this study would lie in guiding the trainers of the teachers and the nursery assistants (the majority of whom are nursery nurses holding the NNEB* qualification). Specifically any discrepancies between actual activities and stated or accepted aims were seen to be of vital interest. More recently the Management Committee expressed the further wish that the project report should be addressed to the widest possible audience: implicitly, the teachers and assistants themselves. Throughout the study, we, the researchers involved, have been constantly aware of an abiding interest in the contrasts between the aims, roles and deployment of the two groups of professionals – in any consistent differences between what nursery teachers generally did and what nursery assistants generally did. Since these groups of professionals start out from very different educational levels, arrive at the nursery by very different training routes, and are paid substantially different salaries, what they characteristically do and what their responsibilities are, is of much more than mere academic interest.

---

*NNEB: National Nursery Examination Board. This qualification is discussed in detail in Chapter 2.

References

1. DEPARTMENT OF EDUCATION AND SCIENCE (1972). *Education: a Framework for Expansion.* London: HMSO (Cmnd 5174).
2. For example McMILLAN, M. (1919). *The Nursery School.* London: Dent; and BOARD OF EDUCATION (1933). *Report of the Consultative Committee on Infant and Nursery Schools.* London: HMSO.
3. For example Social Science Research Council: EPA Action Research Programme; National Foundation for Educational Research: Pre-School Project, and Social Handicap and Cognitive Functioning in Pre-School Children, Phases 1 and 2; Schools Council: Compensatory Education Project.
4. WOODHEAD, M. (1976). *Intervening in Disadvantage: a Challenge for Nursery Education.* Windsor: NFER
5. TIZARD, B. (1974). *Pre-School Education in Great Britain: A Research Review.* London: SSRC.
6. CENTRAL ADVISORY COUNCIL FOR EDUCATION (1967). *Children and their Primary Schools.* London: HMSO.
7. PARRY, M. and ARCHER, H. (1974). *Pre-School Education.* London: Schools Council/Macmillan.
8. TAYLOR, P.H., EXON, G. and HOLLEY, B. (1972). *A Study of Nursery Education.* London: Schools Council/Evans /Methuen Educational.

Chapter 2
Nursery Teachers and Nursery Assistants: Training and Tradition

Professions are moulded by training and tradition. Tradition is concerned with a continuity of values, attitudes and knowledge. Training, though always strongly influenced by tradition, is also the means by which novelty may deliberately be introduced, and thus has a radical function in both promoting and lending direction to professional development and evolution.

In common with that of non-graduate teachers in other spheres, the initial course for non-graduate nursery teachers at present consists of three years training in the theory and practice of education. College of Education requirements are that students must be at least 18 years of age on or before the 1st of October of their year of entry, and possess a minimum of five GCE O-levels. (The academic requirements of individual colleges may be higher.) Nursery courses are often combined with infant or infant and junior courses, and, as a result, nursery teachers have often had experience in teaching older children.

Theory of education courses generally include: theory and philosophy of education; child psychology; health and hygiene; history of education; educational organization and administration; curriculum studies; and at least one field of further study selected from a variety of options.

Practical work in schools usually takes the form of a block of several weeks duration in each year of training, plus odd days for specific purposes, such as observation, child study etc. An intending nursery teacher may spend up to two of her three practices with other age groups.

While training establishments can vary in the interpretation of specific areas of the course, some college staff stress the importance of giving the student an understanding of the role of the NNEB in nursery education and of co-operation with parents. The combination of nursery with infant training has been cited as advantageous in that it gives the student a wider understanding of the developing child, as well as a very necessary flexibility within available job-opportunities.

There are a variety of teacher-training courses currently offered by training institutions which are suitable for nursery teachers as alternatives to the three-year college of education Certificate course. These include:

BEd course: usually four years, but some offer a three-year ordinary course, with an extra year for honours.
PGCE: one-year course for graduates.

Concurrent with this research project (1975-78), economic stringency combined with a falling birthrate have led to the closure or amalgamation of many colleges, and an increase in the number of education departments in polytechnics.

Many educationists, both trainers and teachers, stress the importance of in-service training as a vital supplement to initial training in the light of on-going experience in the classroom.

The James Report[1] recommended that teachers should be released for the equivalent of one term in seven years' service, and aimed at the release of three per cent of the teaching force annually by 1981. At present this seems a remote ideal. However, in-service courses are provided for practising nursery teachers, and in some cases for nursery nurses in the education service, by the Department of Education and Science or by local education authorities and colleges of education. They vary in form from day-release to vacation schools or after-school lectures, and range in duration from one evening to a year. The programme of in-service training attempts a balance between the personal interests of the practitioner and the needs of particular schools. Provision is various, and courses of specific interest to nursery staff range across: interest in particular nursery activities (e.g. music, art and craft, the use of books etc); child development; conversion course for teachers with training in non-nursery age groups; preparation of practising teachers for promotion; and instructing overseas students in the workings of the British education system. In some areas, school-based courses are organized in addition to those of a theoretical nature.

The tradition to which today's nursery teacher is heir may be traced back to Froebel and the spread of the kindergarten idea to this country in the 1870s. By 1900 an estimated 43 per cent of children aged three to five were attending school, either in Board schools which they could attend if they wished, or in private kindergartens and infant schools. But classes were often over-crowded, and in 1905 the right to refuse entry saw the beginning of a long decline in educational provision for the under-fives.

The McMillan sisters, Rachel (1859-1917) and Margaret (1860-1931), struggled for years to focus attention on the importance of early diagnosis of children's ailments, and in 1914 Rachel started an open-air nursery school in Deptford for two- to five-year-olds. The sisters emphasized basic health as a foundation for the full develop-ment of the child, and Margaret's efforts to train teachers in the school led eventually in 1930 to the establishment of a teacher training college.

Maria Montessori (1870-1952) stressed the importance of provid-ing young children with a stimulating environment. She ran short training courses for teachers, and in 1912 the English version of her book *The Montessori Method* made an immediate impact.

The term 'nursery school' seems first to have been used officially in 1908,[2] when it was recommended that nursery schools should be set up in areas of greatest social need. But the long years of economic depression leading up to the Second World War saw a steady decline in the numbers of children getting any kind of nursery education. In 1933, when only about 13 per cent of three- to five-year-olds were attending nursery schools (both Board and private), the Hadow Report[3] suggested that the nursery school provided 'satisfactory conditions for the nurture and education of little children between the age of two and five'. The report recommended that each nursery school should have at least one qualified teacher whose training had included nursery education. Of her qualities, the report said: 'Natural gifts are not enough; such work as hers will demand wide and thorough theoretical knowledge and also the ability to apply this knowledge in actual experience with particular children.' Hadow also stressed that 'the training of the nursery school or class must be carried into the home by active co-operation with the parents of the children'. The report's conclusion was that 'the establishment of a nursery school may be expected to have a beneficial influence upon other schools, and to provide also a centre in which problems connected with the general development and "nurture" of children may be investigated'.

But provision was to remain non-statutory, being left to each authority to make provision according to its perceived needs. Even the good intentions of the 1944 Education Act were not implemented in the nursery sector because the resources available for the statutory age groups were so strained. The standstill in nursery provision continued into the 1960s, when a slight increase in the number of nursery places available in 1964 resulted in priority being given to the children of teachers who were returning to work to alleviate the then shortage in that profession.

The Plowden Report (op.cit.) made recommendations similar to those of Hadow, stressing in particular the importance of parental interest and co-operation. The primacy it gave to 'educational priority areas' was intended to improve the provision of nursery as well as primary schools. Nursery groups should consist of 20 children, with a ratio of at least one qualified teacher to 60 children, supported by trained assistants in the ratio of one to 10 children. Children should attend half-days, unless their circumstances warranted full-time places, and half the full-timers should be in Educational Priority Areas, as defined in the report.

Two eminent practitioners[4] in present-day nursery education summarize tradition in relation to nursery teachers' function thus: 1. encouraging healthy growth and development of children between the ages of two and five; 2. identifying and alleviating (through referral to specialists where necessary) physical and psychological impairments; 3. supporting and counselling parents.

They also stress the fact that many nursery teachers are the leaders of teams. So in addition to her work with the children in the areas of their intellectual, social, moral, emotional and physical development, the teacher has also ascribed roles: of diagnosis, counselling and leadership.

The majority of nursery assistants are nursery nurses possessing the Certificate of the National Nursery Examination Board (NNEB). This is awarded on successful completion of a two-year training course, entry to which is open to anyone (male applicants have been accepted since 1974) of school leaving age, and to older applicants. They should have the personal qualities and aptitudes to profit from the theoretical and practical training. Method of selection is at the discretion of the college offering the course, and is usually based on interview, school report, GCE or CSE examination results and/or one of the generally recognized tests of basic ability. Shorter courses are available for suitable older students aged 23 years or over. The training incorporates the care of children from birth to seven years. There are no nationally laid down minimum entry qualifications, individual colleges setting their own entrance examinations, or alternatively generally accepting candidates possessing four GCE O-levels.

The content of the NNEB course is centrally laid down in general terms, and all colleges wishing to offer the course have to gain NNEB approval. The essential components of the course are: 1. child development and education; 2. health; 3. social element; 4. non-vocational studies, covering related general studies, i.e. home and society, man and his environment, communications and the creative arts (unlike the sometimes non-related specialist subjects of students engaged in teacher training, these three areas of study are related to the rest of the NNEB training).

The specialist skills required of those involved with training necessitate there being within the college staffing complement nursery teachers, health visitors and social work tutors.

Practical experience during training is acquired through placements in either LEA or Social Services establishments. Familiarity with the practical side of hospital work is given to students through visits and short-term stays.

Many colleges providing the NNEB training course also offer in-service courses. A survey carried out recently by the NNEB reported that the types of courses offered included: general refresher courses, encouraging the language development of young children, the care of children with special needs and children in ethnic minority groups. At the present time the Board is seeking the advice of the LEA and Social Services departments on the desirability of the NNEB giving a lead in the promotion of in-service courses, and on the nature and extent of in-service needs in different parts of the country. In a context of increasing inter-departmental co-operation, several local authorities have set up liaison committees or working panels, and through these offer in-service support to all concerned with pre-school provision – teachers, nursery nurses, health workers, social workers, child minders, playgroup personnel and parents. This support includes regular meetings, lectures, short-term and evening courses.

In direct contrast with nursery teachers, whose training is for work in schools (though not necessarily only nursery schools), nursery nurses holding the NNEB qualification may work with young children in a variety of settings: Local education authorities, in nursery, infants or special schools; Social Services Departments, in day or residential nurseries, or as 'home visitors'; health authorities, in maternity wards, special care baby units, paediatric units etc; playgroup associations, in the capacity of supervisor or adviser; Private organizations, in companies' own day nurseries or crèches, those on board ships, within airports etc; Private families, as nannies.

Their tradition thus derives from these different fields of practice, each represented on the National Nursery Examination Board when it came into being in 1945. Changes in the Board's constitution and organization over the years have included its initial expansion to allow greater representation by central government, local authority departments and a variety of allied associations, and the gradual movement towards the Board achieving its own administrative independence, which has now been completed (1978).

References

1. DEPARTMENT OF EDUCATION AND SCIENCE (1972). *Teacher Education and Training.* London: HMSO.
2. *'Report upon the attendance of children below the age of five.'* In: KENT, J. and KENT, P. (1972). *Nursery Schools for All.* London: Ward Lock Education.
3. BOARD OF EDUCATION (1933). *Report of the Consultative Committee on Infant and Nursery Schools.* (Hadow Report). London: HMSO.
4. ROBINSON, A. and BANBURY, J. (1976). *'Is your nursery teacher really necessary? Birmingham Educational Development Review*, No.19.

Chapter 3
*The Nurseries and Staff in the Study**

The local authorities

The 11 local authorities from which the 40 nurseries studied were drawn were all in the south of England. Five were in the Outer London area, and the rest were counties with a mixture of urban, semi-urban and rural areas. Nursery educational provision varied from well below (1.3 per cent) to well above (17.1 per cent) the average for England and Wales (an estimated 7.1 per cent of the population aged three to four) in January 1975. The project methodology specified several protracted visits to each nursery. In order to avoid undue expense, in particular the cost of overnight accommodation, only local authorities within reasonable travelling distance of the NFER in Slough were included. A further constraint imposed was that they should not concurrently be involved in any other nursery research project.

The nurseries

Of the 40 nurseries studied, nine were nursery schools and 31 were nursery classes attached to primary schools. This proportion of schools to classes reflected the national picture at the time of the study.

Because of the implications for the work of the nursery staff and the organization of the nursery it was felt to be important to distinguish between nursery classes with one teacher (henceforth

---

* The information in this chapter is derived from ARD:5, ARD:6, ARD:9 (Appendix A).

called a 'class') and nursery classes with more than one teacher (henceforth called a 'unit'). *The nurseries studied thus consisted of nine schools, five units and 26 classes.*

Their buildings

There was considerable variety in buildings, ranging from pre-fabricated bungalows put up during the Second World War to modern purpose-built nurseries with plenty of light and space. Some were occupying large houses of two or three storeys, or former primary school buildings which had been vacated for newer premises elsewhere. Others were in classrooms within primary schools.

In the case of nursery classes and units, facilities such as playgrounds, toilets, cloakrooms and dining-areas were sometimes shared with children in the primary schools, though many of them had their own independent facilities in the nursery area and their own garden too. The nature of the building and the independence or otherwise of facilities clearly have important implications for the work of the staff and the organization of the children.

'Open' or 'closed'

The grouping of children in the nursery is governed to a considerable extent by the structure of the building: groups may be based in separate buildings, in separate rooms, or at separate ends of the same room. The building may be open-plan, or subdivided by walls and closed doors. The groups may thus mix freely all the time, some of the time, or not at all. The nurseries were designated as 'closed' if groups were segregated by separate buildings, or rooms, for some or all of the time. All other nurseries were designated 'open'. *There were 10 closed and 30 open nurseries in the study.*

Daily programme

In the nursery the daily programme may be scheduled or flexible. Activities such as outdoor playtime, formal group time (music, story) and milk time were used as indicators of flexibility. If two or more of these were allotted fixed times, the daily programme was called 'scheduled', and when less than two were so fixed, 'flexible'. *Thirty-one nurseries in the study had a scheduled daily programme; nine had a flexible programme.*

Staff rota

In some nurseries the staff work to a regular rota, taking set turns with such duties as supervising the garden, taking formal group time, preparing milk and lunch. *Sixteen nurseries in the study worked to a staff rota, and 24 did not.*

The nursery staff

One teacher and one assistant in each of the 40 nurseries were involved in the study. All of them were women.

The majority (33 of each) were married, and had children of their own (24 teachers, 25 assistants).

Initial training

Thirty-six of the teachers possessed a teachers' certificate. Three were graduates possessing a post-graduate certificate of education (PGCE), and one had gone straight from university into teaching without a course of teacher training.

Half the teachers in the study had trained after 1960, when the three-year teacher training course was introduced. Of the remaining 20, two had done 'emergency' one-year courses during the years immediately following the Second World War. Twenty-eight of the 40 teachers had had at least *some* nursery training initially. Of the remaining 12, six had taken a 'conversion' course. The majority of teachers who trained for nursery work had done a combined nursery/infant course, probably mirroring the fact that by the end of 1975 only 14 colleges were offering a nursery course, compared with 73 offering nursery/infant, nursery/infant/junior, or nursery/first-school training.

Thirty-six of the assistants were qualified (NNEB) nursery nurses. Of the remaining four, one was currently taking an NNEB course for mature students, one was a State Enrolled Nurse, and one was a Child Care Reserve. Only one possessed no formal qualification.

None of the assistants in the sample had trained before the NNEB came into existence in 1945. More than half (22) had trained after 1965.

In-service training

In the three years prior to the study, more than twice as many teachers as assistants had attended courses. Some assistants complained that either nothing was provided for them, or that they were not included when information on courses was circulated. In the case of courses which take place during school hours, it is not usually practical for more than one member of staff to be away from the nursery, and the teachers had generally been given preference. In-service provision had varied between the local authorities, some of which also organized regular discussion groups for all nursery staff.

Staff age and status

The 80 nursery staff involved were spread across the full range of employable age, from under 20 to 55 years and over. The largest group were aged between 35 and 44.

The ages of the teachers in the sample probably reflect to some extent their status as heads of nursery schools, and teachers-in-charge of units or classes. As might be expected, 24 of the 28 teachers aged 35 and over, were heads or teachers-in-charge. However, teachers-in-charge were distributed across the whole age range, probably because in a primary school the nursery class teacher does not necessarily hold a scale post. The award of scale posts seemed to vary between authorities and from school to school; most class teachers in the sample who had such a post were aged 45 and over.

All five teachers-in-charge of units had a scale post, and four of them were aged 35 and over.

Many of the assistants expressed the opinion that, while they would prefer to work in hospitals, day nurseries or residential care, where promotion prospects are more clear-cut, they found school work more convenient because the hours they worked fitted in with bringing up their families. When their own children were grown up they could seek employment in the sphere of care and welfare. If assistants are in fact doing this, it could well account for the comparatively small number included in the study who were over the age of 44.

Staff experience

About half of the teachers and of the assistants had had more than 10 years experience of working with children, though not necessarily of nursery age. Of the teachers, only 10 had had solely nursery experience. The rest had had some experience with older children, mainly of infant age. Some of them commented that this had enabled them to have a clearer view of goals for their nursery pupils since they were more aware of what would be required of the children later on.

Twenty-five of the assistants had had experience in two or more other areas of nursery work; only one had experience of no other area. Those who had had infant school experience had mostly qualified since 1965 when practical training in the five to seven age group was introduced. Other experience with young children included working in playgroups and as private nannies. Approximately half the assistants had had working experience in day nurseries and hospitals.

The majority of staff studied had spent not more than five years in their present appointment, though 10 had worked for more than 10 years in the same post.

Only two teachers and one assistant were not full-time, each being employed for five sessions per week.

The children

A total of 2,135 children, 1,763 being part-time and 372 full-time, were involved in this study.

The 40 nurseries ranged in size from 20 to 60 places. As one might expect, most of the classes were 20 to 30 places, whereas most of the nursery schools and units were larger than this.

Most of the nurseries took some part-time pupils, i.e. children who attended for either the morning or afternoon session but not both.

In 18 nurseries all the children were part-timers, whereas in only two nurseries (one class and one unit, both in the same authority) all the children attended all day. The remaining 20 nurseries took both part-time and full-time children, the full-time places generally being allocated to priority cases. The presence of full-time children has important implications for the nursery routine and for the work of the staff. The main influence is the provision of a midday meal. This involves the staff in such duties as supervising children's toileting and hand-washing, supervising and/or sharing the meal, and looking after the children during the after-lunch period, which may involve supervising rest time or play. The provision of school meals usually entails the employment of ancillary staff to cope with the preparation of the meal or to assist with the supervision of the children. The lunchtime routine necessitates the use of a rota and reduces the rest time of the staff. In some part-time nurseries also, meals were provided for children who required them from either session.

Eleven of the schools were situated in urban areas where there were 'pockets of disadvantage' of one kind or another.

In five nurseries the children came from a variety of ethnic groups, and in these the prevalence of English as a *second* language was seen by staff to be an important influence on their work.

The age of the children

The DES Circular No. 2/73 (January, 1973) states that the objective for nursery provision is 'to make nursery education available for children whose parents want it from the beginning of the term after their third birthday, until the term after their fifth birthday'. However, the age range of the children in any one nursery depends on a number of factors such as the time and frequency of intake, age of entry, and age of transfer to the primary school. The ages of the children in this study also depended upon the time of the academic year in which they were visited, as the study progressed.

The median age (i.e. the half-way point in the range of children's ages) at the time of observation for each school was calculated, since it was considered that this could be an important influence upon the work of the staff. More than half the schools had a median pupil age of between four and four and a half. Local policy, which varied between authorities, affected this. Where rising-fives were admitted to infant reception classes, or conversely where the policy was to keep children in the nursery until they were five, the number of places available to younger children was obviously affected and the age-composition of the nursery also.

Staff-child ratios

In 1973 a ratio of staff (i.e. teachers and nursery assistants) to children of 1:13 was described as 'generally acceptable' (DES Circular 2/73). Thirty of the nurseries came within this level.

The same circular expressed the hope that by 1982 'the proportion of qualified teachers would account for at least one half of the total staff'. This would imply a ratio of one teacher to 26 children. In fact, 25 of the nurseries already met with this recommendation.

Constraints

Various characteristics of the nurseries were seen by the 80 staff as being *constraints* on their actions of a more or less severe nature. Each was asked (ARD:10, Appendix A) to indicate the degree (not at all; some; major) to which these eight factors were a constraint upon their work:

Characteristics	*Some*		*Major*		
	Ts.	*Assts.*	*Ts.*	*Assts.*	*Total*
Location of school	4	1	2	1	8
Buildings and facilities	12	20	13	6	51
Staff ratio	6	1	4	2	13
Own status	10	10	0	3	23
Training	17	7	4	2	30
Children (ethnic, social problems etc).	4	3	1	0	8
Inside-school pressures	17	11	5	4	37
Outside-school pressures	8	9	3	1	21

Buildings and facilities was the factor most often rated as a constraining influence. The size and use of indoor space was felt to cause most problems. Many staff would have preferred more space for table activities and floor toys, areas for display and 'wet' activities, and extra rooms for quiet activities and talking with parents. Some of these staff were working in buildings which were not intended for nursery education (22 of the 40 sample schools had not been purpose-built), ranging from three-storeyed houses to war-time day nurseries. High windows and long corridors presented problems of adequate supervision, and sometimes a superfluity of space which was ill-organised was considered as irksome as a building which was too small.

Facilities most often mentioned were toilets which were at a distance from the nursery or were antiquated, and the absence or inaccessibility of a place for the children to do cooking. Shortage of equipment was also mentioned frequently, inevitably limiting the range and variety of children's activities.

The size and layout of the outdoor area of the nursery was also felt to be limiting on children and staff. Improvements most often desired were: adequate fencing to make the garden safe; a grassed area, instead of all tarmac; a level area for climbing apparatus; a covered area for use in wet weather; and more shade, and better drainage.

Gardens which were not adjacent to the classroom, or which were irregular in shape, posed problems of supervision. Several staff felt the irksomeness of having no garden store and of having to carry large toys and heavy equipment from indoors. In some cases the repair of broken toys and apparatus was difficult, though in many schools staff coped with maintenance themselves or enlisted the help of willing parents.

However, it must be pointed out that staff in some nurseries were quite satisfied with the adequacy of their buildings, facilities and equipment, even when these were not particularly new, asserting that the work which goes on in a nursery is more important than gleaming surroundings.

Inside-school pressures was the constraint second in order of mention. It consisted of effects of internal policy, philosophy and organization.

Most often mentioned (by 18 staff) was the influence of the primary school upon the nursery. Staff in nursery classes or units attached to primary schools sometimes felt restricted by the school's timetable. Nursery children were often required to arrive and leave at times to coincide with the older pupils, and outside play and musical activities had to be timed to minimize the effect of noise upon the rest of the school. The exclusion of nursery children from school events such as trips and outings was also a source of displeasure to staff and children alike.

The primary head's policy on the selection, admission and turnover of children in the nursery class sometimes gave rise to problems. Some nursery teachers would have liked more say in such policy, and more information on the background of their pupils. Other points, such as the number of nursery places being too large or small for efficiency, the allocation of younger children to the afternoon session, and the proportion of full-time pupils, were also cited as policy constraints.

The head's philosophy was felt to be important, particularly where it was unsympathetic to, or at variance with, that of the nursery staff. The discouraging of parents, the encouraging of too many visitors, and attitudes to the nursery programme and routine (too rigid or too flexible) were specifically mentioned.

More than half the teachers in the study felt some degree of limitation imposed by their initial training. Positive criticisms most commonly made were that courses had given them insufficient training in classroom management, control and organization; child-care, health and social welfare; specialism in the three to five age group; and working with other staff in a team situation.

Time of training appears to be linked to only one of these criticisms. Teachers who wanted more specialisim in the nursery age-group had all trained since 1965.

Most of the nursery assistants felt that their training was adequate for the work they were currently doing. The most common suggestions for improvements in the NNEB courses were that there could have been a larger component dealing with the *cognitive* development of the child, as well as more on health education and first aid. Those who expressed dissatisfaction felt that their course had not adequately prepared them for work in the education service, or that the age range they had covered was too broad (e.g. nought to seven).

Several assistants felt that it should be easier for someone already possessing the NNEB certificate to acquire a teaching qualification. Both teachers and assistants felt that they should be trained to be more aware of each other's skills and qualifications.

Negative views about their own status were expressed by both teachers and assistants. Many felt that career opportunities for possessors of the NNEB certificate were inadequate, and that nursery assistants thus qualified should have more recognition and better remuneration. It was also felt that not only should the teacher in the nursery be suitably trained for that age group, but that the heads of primary schools with nursery classes should be required to attend a nursery course (as some in fact had done). Some teachers were concerned that their colleagues in primary schools should not regard the nursery class as 'a soft option', or as the training-ground for inexperienced infant teachers.

Chapter 4
Activities and Planning

There are three elements which make up the characteristically informal context of learning in the nursery: the resources, the children, and the staff. A consequence of the traditional commitment to informal, non-directed learning is that there is generally very little explicit organization of these elements, either in space or in time.

The nursery resources – materials and activities – are perhaps the most organized aspect of the nursery classroom, and it is around these that nursery life revolves. For most of a nursery session, a wide range is available to the children. The specific activities made available are varied from day to day, and these activities, between which children are generally given almost total freedom of choice, are supplemented by slightly more formal sessions – stories, music, or milk, for example. There is rarely anything remotely resembling a detailed 'timetable' in the 'school' sense.

In addition to this freedom of access to activities, children are also allowed to choose for how long, and, within 'sensible' limits, for what purpose, they use them. As a consequence of this general freedom, there is also a considerable flexibility in the grouping of children; they may at any time be working individually, in small groups, either co-operatively or associatively (in 'parallel') sharing resources, and in large groups called together from time to time by the staff.

The various aspects of this study involved six half-day sessions being spent in each nursery. On all six occasions, irrespective of the other purposes of the visit, a checklist (ARD:4, Appendix A) was

Summary of activities available

Over all nursery types	%	Schools	%	Units	%	Classes	%
				Within each nursery type			
Books	98	Books	100	Books	100	Playcorners	97
Playcorners	98	Playcorners	98	Playcorners	100	Investigation	97
Investigation	98	Investigation	98	Investigation	100	Books	97
Puzzles/Table Toys	95	Painting/Printing	98	Puzzles/Table Toys	97	Puzzles/Table Toys	94
Painting/Printing	94	Puzzles/Table Toys	94	Sand	97	Sand	94
Sand	92	Water Play	94	Painting/Printing	93	Painting/Printing	92
Floor Toys	90	Wheeled Toys/Apparatus	93	Floor Toys	93	Floor Toys	90
Water	88	Floor Toys	87	Water Play	90	Story/Rhymes	87
Story and Rhymes	87	Story and Rhymes	87	Wheeled Toys	90	Construction Toys	86
Wheeled Toys/Apparatus	86	Construction Toys	85	Story and Rhymes	90	Water Play	85
Construction Toys	84	Sand	85	Colouring/Drawing	73	Wheeled Toys/Apparatus	83
Colouring/Drawing	80	Plastic Play	85	Construction	70	Colouring/Drawing	79
Plastic Play	74	Colouring/Drawing	78	Plastic Play	67	Plastic Play	71
Collage/cutting etc.	56	Collage	61	Collage	57	Collage	55
Music Corner	44	Music Corner	57	Music Corner	57	Music Corner	37
Music	38	Music	46	Junk Modelling	40	Music	36
Junk Modelling	23	Junk Modelling	24	Music	33	Junk Modelling	20
Primary School Skills	17	Primary School Skills	15	Drama	17	Primary School Skills	19
Television	15	Woodwork	13	TV & Visiting Speaker	10	TV & Visiting Speaker	19
Woodwork	15	TV & Visiting Speaker	7	Outings	10	Outings	19
Outings	14	Drama	4	Primary School Skills	7	Woodwork	18
Drama	10	Cooking	2	Cooking	3	Drama	12
Cooking	8	Outings	2	Woodwork	NIL	Cooking	11

(all percentages rounded to the nearest whole number)

completed, recording all the activities made available to the children.

From the aggregation of the 240 resulting checklists, it was possible: i) to see how often each activity was provided in nurseries, *overall;* ii) to see what *proportion* of all activities was generally made available, both overall, and within each type of nursery.

There was very little difference in the number of activities generally made available by the three types of nursery, each tending to make about half of those on the checklist available to the children in each session. Also as the summary table on p.33 shows, the 'top 10' most prevalent activities were more or less the same for each, the first three activities across all types representing what might be called the permanent features of the nursery classroom: the book corner; the imaginative play corner (Wendy house, hospital, shop), and the investigation and discovery area (colour and interest table and nature table).

There are activities that inherently need space either in their provision or use, with some wholly dependent upon there being adequate storage facilities. For example space is needed in a nursery to accommodate a piano, record player, music corner or to keep various pets; messy activities such as clay and dry sand need their own areas, and freedom of movement is necessary in family play and dressing-up. Adequate storage space for cartons, egg crates etc. determines whether junk modelling is possible.

The majority of these activities were more prevalent in nursery units than in either of the other nursery types. By project definition (having at least two teachers on the staff), the units in the study were larger establishments than classes: all were self-contained, having their own facilities.

Nursery units and schools were generally similar in how often they provided space-demanding activities. Such differences that there were seemed to reflect the nature of their buildings. The majority of schools in the study were classified as operating within a 'closed' grouping system. This reflects the home-based grouping of children in almost independently functioning rooms. Units were generally 'open'. Attempting to provide as wide a variety of activities as possible within a single confined area could result in a reduction of the number of activities of a *similar* nature. This is illustrated, for example, by pianos, record players and music corners in schools.

'*Going out to play*' for nursery children can mean anything from being able to use a portion of the primary school playground at set times during the day to having the unrestricted use of a large garden. It would seem that these very different outdoor facilities could account for the fact that classes provided pedal toys much less frequently than both schools and units. In addition, as mentioned in 'constraints' (Chapter 3), the lack of an outdoor shed or store for garden toys limits their availability. The association of gardens with nursery schools, rather than units or classes, probably accounts for mud and soil play being almost totally confined to them.

The attachment to a primary school implicit in the designation 'nursery class' was frequently associated with the provision of 'reading' as an activity and the presence of weather charts and calendars. It also seemed to ensure more 'outings' for the nursery children.

The *planning* of the programme of activities in the nursery was seen to be the responsibility of the teachers. Evidence for this is derived from the questionnaires to head teachers and teachers-in-charge (ARD:8) and to teachers and assistants (ARD:7), which are discussed in detail in chapter six.

Planning was not included in the aspects of nursery life directly observed in this study, the main reason being that it is generally a somewhat diffuse activity. The discussion of it here is based on comments made by staff during informal interviews.

As might be expected, head teachers and teachers-in-charge felt they had the ultimate responsibility for planning what went on in their nursery (Appendix B, Table 1), the latter being constrained to some extent within the administrative framework of the primary school.

In some nurseries, staff planning discussions were carried out on an informal basis at the beginning and end of the day and during lunch breaks. Very few nurseries held regular formal staff meetings; formal meetings usually occurred only once or twice a term, at the beginning of term, half-term or at the start of the school year. In general, discussion was between all members of staff unless this was impossible, as for instance in nurseries with full-time children and staff thus having no completely free break in the middle of the day. In only one or two nurseries were there 'teacher-only' as opposed to 'whole-staff' discussion times. The frequency of such discussions reflected the system of planning and type of organization operating in a nursery; for example, the following-through of weekly 'themes' or 'topics' necessitated weekly planning sessions, and greater daily discussion when there was a daily change in staff responsibility for particular areas of activity in the nursery. The presence of students and the planning of their time to cover the activities specified in their syllabus often resulted in increased staff discussion and redistribution of responsibilities between staff.

Since the overall organization of the nursery was the responsibility of the head teacher or teacher-in-charge, the way activities were planned and presented to children reflected to a great extent her own personal philosophy. The variety in the individual attitudes of head teachers and teachers-in-charge could be seen in the variety of planning procedures adopted within the nurseries in the study. These ranged from staff having an overall view of what was to be attempted during a term, engaging in more detailed planning as necessary, to working within an explicit framework of instruction, with displayed lists giving details of what activities should be made available each day and designating staff responsibilities.

In most nurseries, teachers who had responsibility for a group or class of children were free to plan their own group's activities, and in a 'team' situation planning was often associated with designated areas of responsibility. For example an open-plan nursery was divided into two areas: a 'wet and messy activity' half containing the water trough, painting easels, clay or dough activities; the other half housing the book corner, puzzles and tables games. Members of staff were given responsibility for one half or the other, changing over after a set period – daily, weekly, or even half-termly.

The allocation of responsibility for a particular activity was usually in relation to creative art or craft work, and often this would be related to other activities within a common 'theme' or 'topic'. These themes could be in areas of general interest (e.g. time of year or seasonal festivals – Christmas, Easter; natural history; scientific discovery) or used to introduce and reinforce concepts (number; colour; space). For example a colour-based theme could be reflected in the objects displayed on the 'colour and interest table', the water used in water-play or in the colouring of dough or pastry, as the basis for a variety of creative activities and the focal point of group discussion and story. Themes were often followed through on a weekly basis or until it was felt their potential was exhausted.

The pre-planning of creative activities was deliberately not entered into by some nurseries, where it was felt that these should arise out of children's own areas of interest within a free-play situation.

It was apparent that nursery staff had widely differing attitudes towards the organization of activities and children around the nursery. Examples of these attitudes can be seen in the following list of statements made by teachers and nursery assistants, during informal interviews, in response to being asked what they felt children should experience.

The statements listed are summaries of a number of differently expressed but similar attitudes, and are grouped into two main areas: those relating to *provision of activities* and those concerned with *organization of children in relation to the activities.*

Provision of activities

'The nursery should contain as wide a variety of children's activities as possible to stimulate children's interests and stretch their abilities. Provision should be a combination of instruction and exploration through a balance of formal and informal activities.'

'The nursery environment should be a happy one and provide children with a stable, peaceful atmosphere in which they feel secure. Without a sense of security children are unable to cope with other demands.'

'The nursery programme should be sufficiently varied to meet the "individual" needs of children, and there should be a sufficient number of staff in the nursery for them to be able to be aware of these needs and meet them within the development of the *whole* child.'

'During the time children are in the nursery, particular attention should be given to their language development. Oral skills can be encouraged through activities, social conversation, and discussion thus increasing children's ability to express themselves and communicate with others.'

'Nursery activities should be related to each other in such a way that children are able to see how one activity can lead out of another and be aware of a range of possibilities to develop their own ideas.'

'The nursery is responsible for children acquiring basic skills and concepts: knowledge and ability give children the self-confidence they will need when they go on into the primary school.'

'Children's own games and imaginative play are so important: children learning to play cooperatively within their own set of rules.'

'Children should be given an opportunity to engage in activities not always possible at home: e.g. messy, noisy activities and given freedom of movement to be able to express themselves.'

'If possible (especially if a nursery is attached to a primary school), children should be made familiar with some of the activities they will meet when they enter the main school, e.g. assembly, PE etc.'

Organization of children

'A daily routine or programme of activities gives children security and valuable training in social behaviour, learning to cooperate with others etc.'

'An unstructured daily programme can meet the "individual" needs of children, allowing greater freedom to follow children's own interests.'

'There should be order to the day's activities but not monotony – flexibility in a routine encourages enthusiasm and spontaneity.'

'Children should be occupied and actively engaged in activities; a formal approach ensures learning.'

'Children should be encouraged rather than directed towards activities.'

'Activities should be made available and children allowed to choose for themselves.'

'Children should be given freedom of choice as to whether to join a formal group activity, i.e. music, story etc., or continue with their own activity; one form of activity should not be considered more valuable than another.'

'All children should participate in formal group activities: group times are so valuable, encouraging self-discipline in children to be quiet and listen to others, etc.'

'Small groups are a better medium than large formal groups for some activities, e.g. language development and instruction in manual and primary skills etc.'

'Children should be given as much individual attention as possible.'

Chapter 5
The Aims of the Staff

The traditions of nursery education have already been briefly reviewed in Chapter 2 of this report. These traditions exert a powerful influence on the aims of nursery staff.

The aims of nursery education were investigated in a recent major study by Professor Philip Taylor's team at Birmingham (op.cit). It was teachers' aims only which were explored in that study however, whereas this present study is of the work of both of the nursery professions.

The *aims* of the nursery staff involved in this study were investigated by means of open-ended interviews. The schedule used was ARD:10 (Appendix A). The categorization of the information volunteered was thus imposed retrospectively after a careful consideration of what each individual had said.

Statements made seemed to coalesce into four broad areas of aims: social, educational, preparation for school, and linguistic. Teachers and assistants differed slightly in their rank ordering. Assistants generally made fewer statements than teachers in respect of all of them:

Rank Order	Broad Aim	Number of Statements		
		Teachers	*Assistants*	*Total*
1	Social	57	56	113
2	Educational	27	12	39
3	Prep. for School	18	13	31
4	Linguistic	15	9	24
		117	90	207

It is notable that teachers volunteered more than twice as many statements of 'educational' aims as did assistants. However, it is also notable that both types of professional overwhelmingly emphasized 'social' aims. Thus far staff aims reflect those of the teachers in Taylor's study of whom he concluded that they saw the major purpose of nursery education as being '. . . the social education of the young'. (op.cit., p.60.) Further examination of the components of what were summarized as 'social aims', reinforces this agreement:

Social	Teachers	Assistants	Total
To enable child to integrate, be a member of a group	20	17	37
To give child self-confidence, and independence from mother	20	15	35
To create secure environment, and extension of home	8	7	15
To give social training, in manners, dressing, behaving	5	9	14
To give child adult attention, encourage trust in adults	3	4	7
To make child happy		3	3
Meet individual needs	1	1	2
TOTAL:	57	56	113

In rank order of frequency with which they were volunteered, statements which were paraphrased as 'To enable the child to integrate; to be a member of a group', and 'To give the child self-confidence, and independence from his mother', predominated. These entirely agree with Taylor's findings (op.cit., p.31).

It is interesting to note that, whilst there was broad agreement between teachers and assistants in the number of statements of social aims which they volunteered, the assistants appeared to emphasize 'Welfare' type aims more than the teachers did (manners, dressing, behaving).

Teachers volunteered more than twice as many statements of 'educational' aims as did assistants. These statements were paraphrased thus:

Educational	Teachers	Assistants	Total
To give as wide variety of experience as possible	7	5	12
To develop the child's full potential	9	1	10
To provide a rich/ stimulating/ interesting environment	2	1	3
To develop basic skills and understanding	7	1	8
To encourage learning through play	0	3	3
Early diagnosis of learning problems	2	1	3
TOTAL:	27	12	39

Taylor reported that the teachers in his sample rated what he termed 'intellectual' aims second in order to the 'social' aims. Teachers in this present study also rated such aims second in rank order to the 'social' aims. They differed strongly from assistants in terms of frequency with which they volunteered statements which were paraphrased as 'To develop the child's full potential' and 'To develop basic skills and understanding'. It is interesting to consider the contrast between the highest and lowest rated 'educational' aims reported in the light of Taylor's very similar findings from his much larger sample of teachers (op.cit., p.42).

There was broad agreement amongst both types of staff that they had a duty to prepare children for the next stage in education. This broad aim encompassed statements which referred directly to preparation for school and, more indirectly, referred to the need to familiarize children with routines and group discipline.

Preparation for School	Teachers	Assistants	Total
To prepare the child for school	3	5	8
To enable the child to cope with the next stage	4	2	6
To familiarize the child with routine/ carrying out directions/ learning to listen	3	3	6
To develop certain skills needed for school	2	3	5
To create a 'platform for learning'	4	0	4
To make transition from home to school a happy one	2	0	2
TOTAL:	18	13	31

Taylor also reported that his sample teachers considered '. . . that a valid aim for nursery education is to prepare the child for his infant school, to lay the foundations for his future education'. The relative importance of this aim, as seen by his teachers, was low (4.4 per cent of the statements of aims volunteered by his sample teachers). By contrast, approximately 15 per cent of the statements volunteered by nursery staff in this present study were in this area.

Finally, statements of aims concerned with children's language development constituted about 12 per cent of those volunteered. These were paraphrased as follows:

Language Development	Teachers	Assistants	Total
To encourage the ability to communicate/ to stimulate conversation/ to develop language	15	9	24
TOTAL:	15	9	24

They were more often made by teachers than by assistants. Aspects of language development were seen as distinct from and almost independent of aims related to cognitive or intellectual development, and of social aims.

Taylor also reports this distinction in the way his sample teachers viewed language development, citing just over six per cent of statements volunteered (op.cit., p.40).

The number of staff, and therefore of statements of aims, was much smaller in this study than in that of Taylor (536 teachers; 3,020 statements, op.cit., p.39). However the present main focus was on observable actions rather than non-observable intentions, and whilst it was not possible to establish as differentiated a structure of aims as Taylor reported, it is reassuring to note that when the simpler structure reported at the beginning of this chapter is compared with that of Taylor, they are in fairly close agreement. Even more interesting is the way in which they also accord with the traditions of nursery education, generally in the predominance of social aims, volunteered equally by teachers and assistants, and specifically with the traditions of the two professions, teachers volunteering more non-social aims than assistants.

Chapter 6
Staff Role in the Nursery

Aims are usually thought of as expressing the spirit of matters without being at all precise as to the letter. The things which staff are appointed to do, are expected to do, and have undertaken to do in the nursery are necessarily more specific. In order to understand properly what staff do in trying to achieve their aims, it is necessary first to investigate their responsibilities: as *ascribed* by those in authority, and as they themselves *perceive* them.

Ascribed responsibilities were investigated by a questionnaire (ARD:8 Appendix A) which was given to the head teacher or teacher-in-charge of each nursery. It asked them to indicate who was *mainly* responsible for each of a variety of duties and tasks. Parents, students, and ancillary staff, as well as teachers and assistants were included amongst the possibilities.

Perceived responsibilities were also investigated by a questionnaire (ARD:7 Appendix A) common to both nursery professions and addressed to them. It listed the same duties and tasks as the one (ARD:8) to head teachers and teachers-in-charge. Staff were asked to rate the *extent* to which they felt responsible for each, on a four-point scale: not normally engaged in by nursery staff; little or no responsibility; some responsibility; and major or total responsibility.

The content of these questionnaires was decided after a long period of 'immersion' in pre-school provision – pre-school playgroups and day nurseries as well as nurseries – and much informal discussion with the adults involved.

Staff responsibilities seemed to coalesce into eight areas, and the items in the questionnaires were grouped accordingly, as illustrated by ARD:7 (Appendix A). The percentage ascription of responsibilities is reported in detail in both tabular and block graph form in Appendix B.

Over all the nurseries, teachers were allocated greater responsibility for administration, planning, involvement and adult talk; and nursery assistants greater responsibility for welfare and housework. The two areas where the division of responsibility was not so marked were supervision and equipment, particularly in respect of nursery schools.

The difference in the allocation of responsibilities to student teachers and NNEB students was interesting; student teachers tending to be given greater responsibility for planning and involvement, and NNEB students for housework, thus anticipating their future ascribed professional roles.

The two main areas of responsibility for ancillaries were: housework and administration; and across all nurseries, parents were given some responsibility for supervision, welfare, housework and involvement.

In the comparison of the ascribed responsibilities of head teachers and teachers-in-charge, the trend was towards the greater responsibility of head teachers for administration and adult talk, and the greater responsibility of teachers-in-charge for planning and equipment. Across the three teacher types, teachers-in-charge had the highest responsibility for supervision, equalled only by other teachers in units; other teachers in both units and schools were ascribed more responsibility for equipment than head teachers or teachers-in-charge.

The next step was to see how far staff *perceptions* of these responsibilities agreed with differences in ascription. Each of the 80 staff studied had been asked to indicate the degree of responsibility she felt she had for the various areas of work in her own nursery. Items had been scored on a scale ranging from 'little or none' to 'major or total' responsibility. For this purpose the scores of teachers-as-a-group were combined and compared with those of assistants-as-a-group. Differences between the means of each group in respect of each of the eight areas of work were tested for statistical significance.*

---

*The scores were used for comparisons *between* teachers-as-a-group and assistants-as-a-group. In no way should *within*-group comparisons be made between the work areas, since this was not their purpose. The test of significance used was the Wilcoxon Matched Pairs Test.

Area of Perceived Responsibility	Mean Ts.	Mean Assts	Signif
Supervision	19.9	19.2	NS
Welfare	16.6	18.7	p<.001
Housework	24.9	29.0	p<.001
Administration	25.5	17.0	p<.001
Planning	21.5	15.6	p<.001
Equipment	12.2	12.4	NS
Involvement	22.8	19.8	p<.001
Adult talk	30.0	20.8	p<.001

In two areas, supervision of the children and organization of equipment, there was no significant difference between the mean scores, indicating that in general teachers and assistants felt they had similar degrees of responsibility. In respect of the remaining six areas, teachers in general felt they had more responsibility for involvement in children's activities, administration, adult talk and planning, rating each of these areas more highly than did the nursery assistants. The assistants saw themselves as having greater responsibility for the areas of housework and welfare.

There was thus close agreement between the responsibilities *ascribed* to staff and their *perception* of those responsibilities.

It may be interesting at this stage to compare the allocation of responsibilities to student teachers, NNEB students and parents with the comments expressed by nursery staff during discussion, in respect of the advantages, or disadvantages of the presence of these 'extra working adults' in the nursery.

Students were present in 29 of the 40 nurseries, teacher-students in seven nurseries, and NNEB-students in 22.

The responsibility for the supervision of students was considered by staff to be primarily that of the head teacher or teacher-in-charge, assisted by other teachers and nursery assistants, though the latter were likely to be involved only with that of NNEB students. This apportioning of responsibility appears to be in accordance with that of head teachers and teachers-in-charge, who saw themselves as having more responsibility than other members of staff for adult talk, which incorporates the supervision of students, parents and other helpers in the nursery. Teachers and nursery assistants were both assigned some responsibility for the supervision of students, teachers having greater responsibility than assistants.

The main *advantages* of students in the nursery were considered to be: the overall assistance they gave to permanent members of staff; the extra attention that could be given to children resulting from the increased adult-child ratio; the new ideas and approaches students brought with them from their training that were a source of stimulation in the reassessment of habitual practices. The main *disadvantages* were considered to be: the demand student supervision made on staff time; the presence of students resulting in there being too many adults in the nursery, overwhelming and inhibiting children; their inclusion in the working team affecting, through the re-organization of responsibilities, the position and status of permanent members of staff.

In exactly half of the nurseries studied (20), *parents* were sufficiently involved in the work of the nursery to be included in the division of responsibilities between staff. The degree of this involvement varied, parents being free to come into the nursery at any time, assisting in relation to specific areas only (e.g. fund-raising activities or the cleaning and repairing of nursery equipment etc), or coming in and staying in the nursery only when their children were new.

The widely differing attitudes of staff towards parental involvement can be appreciated in the following examples of opposing views expressed:

> 'The nursery fulfils a therapeutic function for parents.'
> 'We are here to help the children, not the parents.'
>
> 'Parents are not used because the class is too small.'
> 'Parents are not used because the class is too big.'
>
> 'We select parent-helpers very carefully.'
> 'Selection would cause jealousy.'
>
> 'Parents are useful to do the odd jobs.'
> 'Parents are useful as fund-raisers.'
> 'Parents are useful when staff are absent.'
>
> 'Co-operation is essential – we must pull the same way.'
> 'Some are more of a hindrance than a help.'

'Parents can come when pupils are new.'
'Parents can come after new pupils have settled in.'

'Parents can help develop their children's interests.'
'It is best to get the children away from their parents.'

Chapter 7

Nursery Staff: Task Definition

Even to the casual observer of a nursery session, it is evident that the staff engage in a wide variety of tasks, encounter a considerable number of adults as well as children, and are frequently distracted or interrupted in what they are doing.

Observation by Method 2 (ARD:2, Appendix A) was designed to produced a sharply defined picture of what each member of staff was doing. It focused on: the duration of each activity; the context of each activity; the frequency of changes of activity; and who initiated each change in activity.

Radio microphones were worn by staff in order that exactly what was said might be overheard in spite of the background noise normal to the nursery, speech being vital for the precise categorization of what was going on. Each member of staff was observed continuously, and any change in what she was doing was recorded. An example of the sheets used for recording Method 2 Observations is included in Appendix A. It takes the form of a five-second by one-minute grid, each line being one minute subdivided into 12 five-second intervals, allowing for the recording of 15 minutes of observation per sheet. Three code symbols were entered at each observation, recording the activity, the context, and the source of initiation.

The 40 teachers and 40 assistants were each the subject of intensive continuous observation for two complete sessions – a morning and an afternoon.

For observation and recording, the activities in the nurseries and the contexts in which they took place were categorized at two

levels: a more *detailed* level for Method 2, the results of which are
described in this chapter; and a more *general* level for Method 1
(which is reported in Chapter 10). The system as a whole appears in
full in Appendix A.

The data from the observations were adjusted (standardized) to
an average session of two and a half hours (9,000 seconds) so that
comparisons between individuals and the two professions in terms
of activities, context, and initiation would be fair.

Staff spent the largest proportion of their time (41 per cent) in
involvement in children's activities. At the other extreme, the time
spent in passive supervision was minimal (1.4 per cent). (It should
be noted here that many staff mentioned in interviews the importance of standing quietly and observing the children, i.e. 'passive
supervision'. They may have felt that, whilst under scrutiny, this
category of activity could be misinterpreted as idleness!) Nearly a
fifth of their time was spent supervising the children. This means
that a total of nearly 60 per cent of their time was taken up with
supervising and involving the children in activities. Approximately
15 per cent was spent conversing with the children (away from
activities), watching them and attending to their welfare. Thus by
far the greatest part of their time was spent with the children. The
day-to-day running of the nursery in terms of dealing with equipment, administration and housework accounted for only about 17
per cent of their time, and the rest was taken up with talking to
parents, visitors and other members of staff (Appendix C, Table
1A).

This breakdown of what staff did was reflected, of course, in the
proportion of time spent in the different context categories (Appendix C, Table 1B). Three quarters of their time was spent with the
children, in the activities already referred to above. Working alone,
which occupied nearly 15 per cent of their day, might be expected
to involve those tasks in which the children were less likely to be
included, such as much of the housework, administration and
organizing of equipment. Time spent with other adults was mainly
taken up with talking, planning and discussion, and attending to
parents and visitors, though sometimes they also shared the administrative, organizational or household tasks with one another.

It is interesting to note that most of what the staff did was
self-directed (Appendix C, Table 1C). Eighty three per cent of their
time was spent in behaviours which were apparently initiated by

themselves, whereas only 17 per cent was seen to be a direct result of a child's or other adult's demand for their attention.

The frequency with which changes of task occurred may best be described as 'fragmentation'. The average number of changes per session (2½ hours) was 175, an average of almost one a minute (Appendix C, Table 2A). As might be expected from the proportion of time overall spent with children, changes occurred most frequently in their context, and least often when with other adults (Table 2B).

Dividing the overall time spent in each category of activity by the frequency of change for each gives its episode duration. In rank order these were:

	Episode: Average duration
Involvement in children's activities	98 seconds
Administration	64 seconds
Housework	62 seconds
Dealing with equipment	53 seconds
Passive supervision	48 seconds
Care and welfare	41 seconds
Conversing with children	35 seconds
Supervising the children	32 seconds
Talking with other adults	29 seconds*

Involvement in children's activities again takes the lead, staff spending an average of just over one and a half minutes each time they became involved in the children's work. In many instances, of course, they spent a good deal longer, telling a story to a group or showing a child how to cut out a shape. (An average being what it is, in many instances they also spent a good deal less than one and a half minutes before turning to other matters.)

Dealing with housework, equipment and administrative tasks lasted on average roughly one minute, about two thirds as long as periods of involvement in children's activities. Of briefest average duration were instances of talking with other adults (which con-

---

*Times rounded to the nearest whole second.

sisted mainly of short asides to colleagues, and the greeting of parents and visitors) and supervision (which often consisted of directing children to specific tasks or briefly intervening to warn, arbitrate or admonish).

To a considerable extent, the uninterrupted time spent in any task behaviour is dictated by the nature of the task. It takes more time to become involved in children's activities than it does to speak briefly with a colleague in passing or to cast a supervisory eye over a group of children. Similarly, most 'household' and administrative tasks necessarily take longer to perform than, say, praising or admonishing a child. In the light of this, an examination of the average period of time spent in each context category is interesting:

Working alone	71 seconds
Working with children	52 seconds
Working with other adults	32 seconds

On average, staff tasks lasted longest when they were working *alone:* perhaps they met with fewer interruptions then!! One might have expected that since involvement in children's activities lasted longest, on average working with children would also have lasted longest. However, the tasks which came second, third and fourth in length (administration, housework and equipment), were all ones where most of the tasks would have to be performed by staff working by themselves, and these could have accounted for the fact that, on average, tasks carried out alone were of longest duration.

Tasks which were initiated by *others* (i.e. instant distractions and interruptions) were shorter than those which staff appeared to initiate themselves.

Looking at durations, frequencies and mean durations together, some interesting patterns emerge.

Involvement in children's activities took up more of staff time than any other category, and also persisted the longest. By contrast, passive supervision took up least of their time and was engaged in fairly briefly.

On the other hand, supervision occurred the most often, more frequently than involvement, but instances did not last long. This was because many instances of supervision consisted of briefly directing children towards some specific task (e.g. 'Put the paintbrush in the sink please Michael'), settling a dispute between two children, or gathering a group together ('Come on then, let's go and feed the rabbit') and so on. But when the member of staff actually got involved with the group in feeding the rabbit, this was categorized as involvement, and the episode could last for several minutes.

In contrast with supervision, administrative tasks occurred least often, although when they did occur they lasted a relatively long time. This was not surprising: although administration took up a minimal part of the day for most people, such tasks as answering telephone calls, marking registers, ordering meals or writing letters necessarily cannot be accomplished in only a few seconds.

Some tasks seemed to be remarkably consistent in respect of all three measures. At the two extremes, involvement and passive supervision were consistently predominant and minimal respectively. The scores for equipment, welfare and conversation also showed consistency across all analyses. The organization of equipment, which took up the third longest part of the day, was the fourth most frequently occurring and the fourth longest in duration. Similarly, care and welfare and conversation with children ranked consistently fifth to seventh.

But the different measures showed interesting irregularities in respect of some tasks. Housework occupied only six per cent of an average day, and accounted for less than five per cent of all instances; nevertheless, when engaged in, it lasted a comparatively long time – almost as long as administration.

Conversely, instances of talking with other adults occurred quite frequently but were of very brief duration.

So, looking at the 80 staff studied, a general picture of an average nursery session emerged, in which: 60 per cent of the time was spent working with the children – supervising and involving them in activities; 20 per cent of the time was taken up by social contacts with the children through conversation, care and welfare, and with other adults in talk and discussion; 20 per cent of the time was occupied in the day-to-day running of the nursery, i.e. tasks involving administration, housework and equipment.

These averages of course, encompass wide variations between individual nurseries, and it is logical to suppose that these variations are attributable to factors related specifically to the staff themselves, to their nurseries, and to the children with whom they worked.

As a method of educational research, observation is much more demanding of researchers' time than most other methods. The number of nursery staff included, one teacher and one assistant in each of 40 different nurseries, was adequate for the main purposes of the study, and was determined at the outset by the choice of structured observation as the principal research method. The nurseries were selected in such a way that they were, *in aggregate*, representative of nurseries in general, and thus conclusions based on data obtained from them are also, *in aggregate*, generalizable. The numbers were not large enough, however, to make a range of statistically valid comparisons by nursery type (school, unit, or class), or *within* the two professions. Such 'sample-splitting' would have required a much larger initial sample, much too large in fact for an observational study with the resources available. There were however two trends in the data worthy of report.

As might be expected, the work of staff was influenced by staff-child ratios. (The DES recommendations on this were noted on page 28.) There was a tendency for involvement in children's activities, particularly with individual children, to increase where the ratio of staff to children was high, and for conversation with children and welfare activities to increase where it was low.

It was also expected that the ages of the children would affect the work of the staff. There was a fairly clear trend in line with this expectation. The younger the children, the more time was spent on welfare, and episodes of all activities were shorter. The older the children, the longer the staff spent on involvement in children's activities, on housework, and on administration. Primary school skills were observed more often, and episodes of all activities lasted longer.

Morning and afternoon sessions seemed to be entirely similar in respect of observed staff activity, with the sole exception that rather more work with large groups of children was done in the mornings.

Chapter 8
Staff Deployment: Teachers and Assistants

The discussion of life in the nursery so far has referred to staff collectively, despite the acknowledged differences in the training, tradition, aims and responsibilities of the two professions. The degree to which these differences are reflected in observed differences in their deployment will now be considered.

For this purpose, the data from Method 2 observations (ARD:2, Appendix A) were re-examined for teachers and assistants in two distinct ways. Firstly a stress was placed on finding out precisely to what degree, and in what ways, the deployment of the two professions *differed*. Then a *description* of deployment typical of each was derived. The difference between differentiation and description will become clearer as the processes are described.

In order to establish the distinctive characteristics of nursery teachers' activities, as compared with those of nursery assistants, the data were submitted to a discriminant analysis.*

Discriminant analysis was first developed for botanical classification. It takes account of the various features of what is being investigated (plants . . . or people), and produces a formula from the combination of features which best distinguishes different classes (of plants, people, or whatever). In doing so it determines the relative importance of each feature to the discriminant function, setting aside and ignoring those which contribute little or nothing to

---

*A detailed explanation is given in Appendix D.

the process of differentiation, thus producing an incomplete description. The 'features' of the teachers and assistants were the overall durations, frequencies of changes and mean durations of episodes of staff activity discussed in Chapter 7.

By combining the overall *durations* of six of the nine summary activities into a discriminant function, 77 per cent of staff were correctly classified, 86 per cent of teachers conforming to the teacher-pattern, and 68 per cent of assistants conforming to the assistant-pattern. The six summary activities were, in order of importance: housework, administration, organization of equipment, adult talk, supervision and conversation with children. The remaining three – involvement in children's activities, welfare and passive supervision – did not significantly contribute to *differentiation* between teachers and assistants, and were therefore discarded from the function (formula) (Appendix D, Table 1).

Turning to description, teachers and assistants spent their time in the following ways:

Summary Activity	Teachers	Assistants
Involvement in children's activities	45%*	38%*
Supervising the children	20%	17%
Talking with other adults	9%	8%
Dealing with equipment	8%	11%
Conversing with children	7%	6%
Care and welfare	6%	7%
Housework	2%	10%
Administration	2%	1%
Passive supervision	1%	2%

*All percentages rounded to whole numbers

It can be seen that both professions did everything from involvement to administration, but that of some things teachers generally did more, of other things assistants generally did more. The teachers as a group spent marginally more time on involvement, supervision, adult talk, conversation with the children and administration, whereas the assistants as a group spent marginally more time on dealing with equipment, care and welfare, and passive supervision, and much more on housework.

Turning to direct measures of *context*, this is with whom they spent their time:

Teachers
Working with children	79% of their time
Working with other adults	11% of their time
Working alone	10% of their time

Nursery Assistants
Working with children	71% of their time
Working alone	19% of their time
Working with other adults	10% of their time

It can be seen that both teachers and assistants spent most of their time working with the children, though on average the teachers spent eight per cent more. This is accounted for by the fact that they spent rather more time on involvement and supervision. The nursery assistants spent significantly more time working on their own than did the teachers, and this is accounted for by them doing more housework and organization of equipment. In respect of both of these, many of the tasks, like cleaning toilets or cutting up paper, are unlikely to be carried out with the children's help.

When 'working with children' was broken down into working with individuals, small groups, or large groups, it was found that the teachers and the assistants spent roughly the same amounts of time with individual children. However teachers spent most time with groups of children, especially with the class as a whole.

When 'other adults' is subdivided into nursery staff and parents/ visitors, the assistants spent more time with other staff (possibly because they often shared responsibility for NNEB students), and the teachers spent more time with parents and visitors.

Both teachers and assistants spent more than 80 per cent of their time in self-directed behaviours and less than 20 per cent responding to the demands of others.

From the *frequency* with which staff were observed to change activities, a discriminant function which correctly classified 83 per cent of staff resulted, 85 per cent of teachers conforming to the teacher-pattern, and 80 per cent of assistants to the assistant pattern. Eight of the nine staff activities were included, in this order of importance: administration, housework, organization of equipment, involvement in children's activities, passive supervision, conversation with children, adult talk and welfare. Only one, supervision, was discarded (Appendix D, Table 2).

It would appear that it is in the nature of nursery work for staff to change from one task to another very frequently. On average, both the teachers and the assistants in the study made about 175 changes of task in a two and a half hour session.

Comparing the two staff groups in rank order of the frequency with which they changed from task to task shows considerable similarity:

Teachers

Supervising the children	31% of all changes
Involvement in children's activities	25% of all changes
Talking with other adults	14% of all changes
Conversing with children	10% of all changes
Dealing with equipment	8% of all changes
Care and welfare	7% of all changes
Housework	3% of all changes
Administration	2% of all changes
Passive supervision	1% of all changes

Assistants

Supervising the children	28% of all changes
Involvement in children's activities	19% of all changes
Talking with other adults	15% of all changes
Dealing with equipment	11% of all changes
Conversing with children	9% of all changes
Care and welfare	9% of all changes
Housework	7% of all changes
Passive supervision	1% of all changes
Administration	1% of all changes

Obviously the number of changes which *can* take place is governed ultimately by the overall duration of each summary activity, as well as by any differential tendency or willingness to change activity on the part of staff. Bearing this in mind, for both groups changes occurred most often in supervision and involvement, and least often in passive supervision and administration. The number of changes when they conversed with and observed the children, or talked with other adults, were similar for both groups.

Changes occurred more often for teachers in connection with children's activities and administrative tasks; for assistants, in connection with housework and equipment. These reflect the differences (described earlier) in how the two groups spent their time.

It is interesting again to note that the dominant summary activity in respect of changes, supervision, was the one which did not contribute to the discrimination between teachers and assistants.

The third measure used to describe staff life in the nursery was episodes (average duration) of the summary activities. The average length of these episodes ranged from about one and a half minutes down to about 30 seconds (page 52), and it was suggested that they were of such brevity as to constitute 'fragmentation'. However, all nine of the activities were included in a discriminant function which correctly classified only 69 per cent of staff, 71 per cent of teachers conforming to the teacher-pattern, and 66 per cent of assistants conforming to the assistant-pattern. The order of importance of the activities in this discriminant function was: housework, welfare, administration, conversation with children, organization of equipment, adult talk, involvement in children's activities, supervision of children, and passive supervision (Appendix D, Table 3).

This was the weakest of the three discriminant functions. In other words, in respect of how long, on average, episodes lasted for each summary activity, teachers and assistants were more similar than they were in respect of how long overall they spent on each activity or how often they changed, or were interrupted.

The rank orders of teacher and assistant activity episode durations were:

Teachers	*Assistants*
Involvement in children's activities	Involvement in children's activities
Administration	Housework
Dealing with equipment	Passive supervision
Housework	Administration
Care and welfare	Dealing with equipment
Passive supervision	Care and welfare
Conversing with children	Conversing with children
Supervising the children	Supervising the children
Talking with other adults	Talking with other adults

Episodes of involvement in children's activities lasted longest, about one and half minutes on average, in the case of both teachers and assistants, and talking with other adults shortest, about half a minute on average. As commented when the duration of episodes of activity for staff combined was discussed (page 52), these averages encompass episodes of a much longer – and a much shorter – duration.

Since staff life in the nursery seems to be characterized by frequent brief episodes of activity, it is considered to be important to provide a fuller portrayal of this measure of staff deployment than can be offered solely by rank orders or averages. To provide such a fuller characterization, block graphs of the distributions of episodes of different durations of each of the nine summary activities are presented in Appendix D.

For two of the activities, conversation with children, and supervision of children, the distributions were bi-modal, that is there were two 'typical' kinds of episode, brief ones lasting from six to 10 seconds and rather longer ones lasting from 16 to 30 seconds. The shorter episodes were generally concerned with sustaining or maintaining children's activities, or the settling of minor problems and disputes. The longer ones, still surprisingly brief, were concerned with redirection.

As might be expected, then, nursery staff were generally observed to be differentially deployed by profession, the sharpness of differentiation varying according to the particular measure used – most in respect of frequency of change of activities, least in respect of duration of separate episodes of activity.

Teachers, on the whole, were the more homogeneous of the two professions, each discriminant function 'correctly' classifying rather more teachers as teachers than assistants as assistants. This tendency for assistants to be less homogeneous as a group – more prone to display behaviour patterns which approximated to those of teachers – is readily explained by the status hierarchy of the nursery, is interesting socially and *may* have educational implications.

However, before too clear a dichotomy is inferred between teachers and assistants, it is necessary to consider the ways in which they differed, and the ways in which they did not.

Although each of the discriminant analyses distinguished teachers from assistants, the summary activities which contributed most to this process were the *domestic* ones – housework, administration and organization of equipment. Of the staff activities which directly included the children, supervision was discarded in one of the three discriminant analyses (as having no contribution to make) and was amongst the weakest retained discriminants in the others. Conversation with children also made a relatively weak contribution to differentiation between teachers and assistants in all analyses. Most important, involvement in children's activities, which is the epitome of the interaction between adults and children in the nursery so valued by educationalists, and which dominated staff life in the nurseries studied, consistently made a weak or negligible contribution to differentiation between teachers and assistants. In simple terms, they did not appear to be differentially deployed in respect of *educational* variables.

It seemed possible that this apparent similarity between teachers and assistants in respect of the educationally important 'involvement in children's activities' was an artefact of the aggregate nature of that summary activity. The specific activities of which it was composed are listed in ARD:2, Appendix A.

Before anyone can become 'involved' in an activity, it has to be available. In Chapter 4 it was reported that about half of the aggregate of activities in the nurseries studied were generally made available in each nursery, each session, and that there was a 'top ten' including such as books, sand and play corners in evidence in almost every nursery and available every session. Others were observed less frequently for two reasons: either they were available often but in only a few nurseries, like woodwork, for example; or they were offered only once or twice a week in most nurseries, as, for example, watching a television programme or doing cookery.

However, availability to the children does not necessarily imply that staff will automatically be involved. Clearly, there are certain activities, such as sand and water play, which are commonly provided but in which the children seem often left to their own devices, whereas other activities like puzzles and table games or specific art and craft skills are deemed to require the presence of an adult for their successful completion.

A comparison between availability of activities and adult involvement in them is given in Appendix D, Table 4. Those activities which were most frequently seen and which might be considered the essential components of the traditional nursery – play corner, book corner, sand, water – took up far less staff attention than did other activities which inherently require more adult direction or supervision.

For five of the 24 activities aggregated in involvement, there were statistically significant differences between teachers and assistants. They were:

> Books: frequency; *
> overall duration; *
> Primary school skills: frequency; *
> overall duration; *
> Wheeled toys and apparatus: frequency; *
> Investigation: frequency; *
> overall duration;
> Stories: frequency; *
> overall duration.

The average duration of episodes of these five activities did not differ significantly for teachers and assistants.

For none of the other activities were there statistically significant differences between teachers and assistants (Appendix D, Table 5).

For the measures marked with asterisks(*), the statistical significance of the differences was $p < .05$, the lowest commonly accepted as worthy of report. In other words, they were poor discriminators between staff. Thus, of the 24 constituents of involvement in children's activities, it was only in respect of the overall duration of investigation and stories that teachers were clearly differentiated from assistants in matters which involved them directly with the children, and which might be characterized as educational.

There remained, however, the possibility that, although there was very close *apparent* similarity between teachers and assistants in respect of measures of *quantity* of involvement in children's activities, there might well be differences in quality. This is examined in the next chapter.

Chapter 9
Adult Speech and Staff Differentiation

For the more detailed of the two observation systems, Method 2, staff and researchers were linked by radio-microphones. This served two purposes: first, it allowed the researchers to hear precisely what was said by the adult so that accurate categorization of task might be achieved; and secondly, it enabled samples of adult speech to be tape-recorded for later analysis alongside the task-behaviours to which they related.

Two aspects of nursery staff speech were studied: adult/adult talk; and adult/child speech. The analysis of adult/adult talk can be described fairly briefly and will be dealt with first.

The staff observed in the study spent on average eight to nine per cent of their time talking with each other and with other adults. The content of adult-to-adult talk was subdivided into talk concerned with administration; housework; equipment; organization of staff; supervision and organization of children; care and welfare; and development of children's abilities and activities.

Teachers engaged most in talk related to nursery administration and to the development of children's abilities and activities. On the other hand, the assistants talked most with other adults about the organization of nursery equipment, as well as administration and children's progress. When talking to parents, the teachers were again more inclined to discuss administrative matters and children's progress. Assistants on the whole talked less with parents than did the teachers, but spent more time talking with NNEB students, for whom they often shared responsibility. It was expected that talk relating to the organization of staff would be carried out mainly by teachers but this was not observed to be the case. Both groups had a small part to play in this, with the teachers only marginally ahead, probably because in close-knit teams the organization of adults is largely implicit, and relates to earlier planning.

The activity-based curriculum is fundamental to nursery education, and involvement in children's activities, not unexpectedly, therefore, turned out to be the major occupation of the nursery staff studied. What could not be understood or even inferred from observation, however, was what *purpose* this general commitment to involvement was intended to serve.

It was therefore decided to consider in detail some examples of the speech of nursery staff and the children with whom they were involved.

Two 15-minute tapes had been made for each session, always at times when the adult being observed was involved in children's activities. She did not know *when* she was being recorded (though it was done with her permission, of course). Thus a collection of some 80 hours of nursery staff speech was built up, consisting mainly of interactions with children during activity time.

Though the concern here was with the speech of the adult, the responses of the children were essential to the sequence of interaction, and because of the sensitivity of the radio microphone it was possible also to record the speech of the children with whom she was talking.

This collection of nursery staff speech would warrant a research study in its own right, but in relation to this project (which was not primarily concerned with linguistic theory and analysis) its use was confined simply to attempting to understand what nursery staff were trying to achieve by the task to which they were so overwhelmingly committed.

The tapes were searched for sequences of speech which took place in relation to those activities for which there were no significant differences between teachers and assistants in respect of duration and frequency, and hence also mean duration (see Appendix D, Table 5), and these were transcribed.

The transcripts were then searched for matched pairs: instances of teacher and assistant from the *same* nursery working on the *same* type of activity. The reason for this was to allow for comparisons *within* pairs working in situations of the closest similarity, as well as between pairs. The activities where matched pairs were available for study were: play corners, table toys, water, plastic play, painting/ printing, collage/cutting and construction. These were searched for sequences of staff speech which were as complete in themselves as possible, e.g. when an adult seated herself beside a child and helped him finish a jigsaw. Sequences contained between 20 and 40 adult utterances.

The final sample for speech analysis consisted of 10 pairs of teachers and assistants (20 adults) in nurseries, reflecting the proportion of classes, schools and units in the main study. Activities which were sampled more than once (e.g. table toys) were those where matched pairs most often occurred. No nursery was sampled more than once. None of the nurseries was known to have recently taken part in any specific language development projects. The sample is tabled below:

Children's Activity	Nursery Type	No. of Utterances (Teachers)	No. of Utterances (Assistants)
Collage/cutting	School	31	28
Collage/cutting	Class	26	30
Table toys	Class	30	30
Table toys	Unit	36	39
Construction	Class	30	36
Construction	Class	35	29
Plastic play	Class	30	32
Water play	Class	30	30
Painting/printing	School	22	20
Play corners	Class	26	22
(TOTAL 7)	(10)	296	296
		TOTAL = 592	

A sample of almost 600 staff utterances within the context of children's activities was thus available for analysis.

Transcripts of the sequences could be studied in conjunction with on-the-spot observation sheets so that the speech could be interpreted within the situation in which it took place. The 20 sequences studied are summarized in Appendix E, Table 1. A full example is given below.

> The setting is a nursery class during activity time. A small group of children are busy at the water tray, trying to make the water pump work. A member of staff joins them.

Adult	Let me see what we've got here. Shall I try and pump some water through it? Has it got a top on? No, it hasn't. Doesn't pump very well then does it?
Child	Is that the top?
Adult	No, it's a little white top. You probably won't be able to see it because it's hidden underneath . . . Oh there it is in there.
Child	That's a top.
Adult	That's the bit that screws on and makes it pump up the water. Do you want me to put it on?
Child	Yes.
Adult	Put it on like that. Then if you pump this, look. You put this bit in the water. Let me show you. That bit in the water and this green bit should pump up. Here it comes. You see, if you pump there it comes through Nita's funnel. Can you see?
Child	I'm going to do it now.
Adult	Can you see it coming through, Julian?
Child	I'm playing with it.
Adult	Yes, well that doesn't come through there 'cos that's tightened up, Sasha. Is that a cup of tea you've got there, Jamie? Can you see the bubbles coming up? Isn't it exciting?
Child	I can see a red thing.
Adult	That's where it's joined on I think. Look at those beautiful bubbles Sasha's made there. Can you see them in the corner? If you take that off it won't pump any more. That stops the air coming through.
Child	You've got too much.
Adult	Overflowing, isn't it. Ooooh. Wipe it on one of these towels here, it will be softer on your nose, look. Those towels are hard, aren't they?

With such a small sample of adults it is important to avoid over-generalization. It is, however, possible to note certain emergent points. Even in this relatively small study, three factors were apparent. One was the *use* the adult made of the activity in which she was involved. The second was the *style* of discourse she employed. The third, which was related to her use of the activity and to her style, was the *complexity* of the speech she used.

1. The use of the activity

One of the distinctive features of the nursery is the flexibility of use which may be made of the variety of available activities. For example the coloured bricks may be used by an individual child to create a construction of his own whim; by a group of children to build a fort as part of their imaginative play; or by a member of staff to help a child understand the principles of matching and sorting.

Interest here was in the uses made by the *staff* of the activities in which they were involved. The 20 staff in the study seemed to fall into two distinct groups: those who were using the activity as an *end* in itself, and those who where using it as a *means* to some other end. For example cutting out pastry shapes: in one sequence this activity was used to encourage the skills of cutting the shapes accurately and lifting them out successfully; in another instance, the same activity in the same school was used by a different adult as the basis for a discussion about stars: star shapes, colours, stars in nursery songs, stars in the night sky and so on. In both cases manipulative skills were important, but in the first case the activity itself remained the focus of attention, while in the second case the activity was used as a starting-point from which the children's attention was drawn outwards beyond the immediate situation. The former could be described as an activity used as an *end* in itself, the latter as a *means* to language development, knowledge and cognitive skills.

In other words, the activity may be used to develop the skills *inherent* in carrying out that activity, or it may be extended to include skills *beyond* those necessary to the activity itself. An example of each is given below.

> In the first extract a small group of children are being shown the skills required to cut out pastry shapes; the activity is used as an *end* in itself.

Child	What's Sarah doing?
Adult	Cutting some shapes out of the pastry. Didn't you do some pastry when you came in Maria?
Child	A rabbit.
Adult	A rabbit. Now if you'd have pressed a little bit harder, you could have got him out whole. Turn it round; now press harder. Now pull the pastry from round the sides. Leave your mould on. That's it. Then you have the rabbit's head left behind. See, when you roll the pastry thinner. Much better isn't it? Not so hard to press down.
Child	Two rabbits.
Adult	Put them on the table then.
Child	You have to give me some.
Adult	Will you get another shape on there? Is there enough pastry? Have to find a small shape to fit on that place. That's it. There, now you have to roll it in a ball with your hands. Put it in a big ball, then roll it out again. That's it, like this, look. Press it all together, then you can start again. You can roll it out thin and make some more shapes. Oh dear, won't it go into a shape? Push your fingers through it, that's it. Now you put it with the other shapes. That's it.

In the second extract, the activity of making pastry shapes becomes secondary to the discussion; the activity is used as a *means* to other ends.

Adult	Oh that really is tiny, isn't it? Couldn't you give him a bit off the edge when you've cut your star out? How many points has your star got Philip?
Child	Four. Four, five.
Adult	Ah, you were one wrong weren't you? Five yes, five points. That's right, pull it out very carefully. There's a lovely star. That's a twinkle, twinkle little star. Only it's green. Stars aren't usually green are they?
Children	No, white.
	Black.
	They're white.

Adult	Black?
Children	No, blue.
	White.
Adult	Sort of blue or silver.
Child	White.
Adult	Yes, white, yes. That's right, roll it out and get it nice and thin.
Child	I've got white.
Adult	You've got white and blue.
Children	I got white.
	And me.
	And red.
Adult	And red, res.
Child	I got a star.
Adult	Are you like a star? But stars twinkle, don't they? Looks like their lights are going on and off. 'tisn't really, but it looks as if it is when you look up to the stars.

In the 20 speech sequences studied, activities were used as follows:

*Activities used as **ends:***

   Table toys: to complete a matching game (teacher)
   Table toys: to complete a matching game (assistant)
   Table toys: to complete a jigsaw puzzle (assistant)
   Plastic play: to cut out pastry shapes (assistant)
   Water play: to work the water pump (assistant)
   Painting/printing: to master the technique of dribble-painting (assistant)
   Collage/cutting: to cut out foot shapes (teacher)
   Collage/cutting: to make paper hats (assistant)
   Collage/cutting: to glue pebbles and shells on a mosaic crown (assistant)

*Activities used as **means:***

   Play corners: imaginative play in the Wendy House to show how to make a cup of tea (teacher)
   Play corners: the shop, to control deviant behaviour and to promote imaginative play (assistant)
   Construction: making a dock, to follow up theme of television

programme (teacher)

Construction: making a dock, to follow up theme of television programme, with reference to pictures in books (assistant)

Construction: house with small bricks to stimulate discussion on child's experiences (teacher)

Construction: Lego cranes and fire engines to stimulate discussion on how real cranes and fire engines work (assistant)

Collage/cutting: mosaic picture to stimulate interest in the Silver Jubilee and provide discussion on Royal Family (teacher)

Plastic play: pastry shapes to stimulate discussion on stars (teacher)

Water play: water pump to demonstrate the action of air in water (teacher)

Table toys: jigsaw puzzle to initiate talk about numbers, comparisons, relationships (teacher)

Painting/printing: sprinkle-painting to initiate talk about colours (teacher)

A total of two teachers and seven assistants were using an activity as an *end*, and eight teachers and three assistants were using an activity as a *means* to a variety of ends. It would be interesting to see whether this distinction between teachers and assistants in the way they used activities would be sustained in a larger sample, and how much of the difference may be attributed to their respective training and traditions.

It must be stressed that both uses of activities are valid in developing the nursery child's potential. It may be argued that some activities lend themselves more to one use than another. For example, in a matching game played with a group of children, attention is more likely to be focused on completing the game (an end in itself), whereas the Wendy House is perhaps more often used as a stimulus for imaginative or symbolic play (an extension outwards from the immediate situation), and these were indeed the case in this small study.

Finally, it must be noted that the use of an activity may or may not have been predetermined by the adult. That is, she may have set out with clear ideas of what she was going to do with the children, e.g. making paper hats; or she may have joined a child who was already busy, say, with the bricks, and used what he was doing as a basis for developing other skills.

2. Styles of staff speech (see Appendix E, Table 2)

The use an adult makes of a nursery activity may be effected through a variety of styles. One member of staff may adopt an approach which is gently encouraging and which builds upon the responses of the children. Another may be more directive, giving the children instructions and explicitly controlling what they are doing. A third may adopt a combination of both approaches.

Much will depend upon the ability of the children to respond as well as on the adult's ability to elicit responses. A noticeable feature in this study was the relatively small number of children's utterances compared with adults' utterances. These ranged from one to 27 utterances per sequence for children, compared with from 20 to 39 for adults. A typical sequence of adult/child speech within an activity went as follows:

No. of adult utterances	No. of child utterances
2	1
9	1
6	1
10	1
1	1
8	1

Much of the children's speech in the sample consisted of single statements or one-word utterances. An example is given below:

Adult	You're very busy here, Arlette. Are you cooking something nice? Are you cooking something for me? Arlette? A nice cup of tea perhaps for me. I'm feeling rather hungry. Jolly good, there's the teapot. What do you have to put in tea? Do you just pour it out of a teapot or do you put anything else with it?
Child	Tea.
Adult	What do we have to put with tea usually, Arlette?
Child	Teapot.
Adult	Well do you just pour it out the teapot and give it to people like that, or is there something else with the tea in the cup? What else is in the cup?
Child	Sugar.

Adult	Sugar. You can put sugar if you like sugar.
Child	And milk.
Adult	And milk rather. Yes, I like . . .
Child	Teabag.
Adult	And a teabag. Well, I don't think . . . Don't you think teabags would be in the teapot?
Child	No.

Children's speech cannot be ignored in a study of staff speech, since the continuity of the interaction depends in part on the response of the adult to the child as well as vice versa. Contrast the extract above with this less typical one:

Adult	What are these parts underneath for?
Child	They're wheels.
Adult	The wheels. Does this move round?
Child	No.
Adult	Oh, that's a lovely one too, Luanne. And is that a crane or a fire engine?
Child	Fire engine.
Adult	Are these the ladders? What's this part here?
Child	Ladders.
Adult	I thought it was.
Child	And this is a ladder to climb up.
Adult	Is it a very high crane? Where is your crane?
Child	Haven't gone one now. I've changed it into a fire engine.
Adult	Changed it into a fire engine? What did you do to change it?
Child	Just lifted it up.
Adult	Just lifted that one up. That's lovely. That's Luanne's fire engine, can you see? And this part is the . . .
Child	Ladders, and that piece is the 'scape and the men can get out of it 'cos that's so they can't and that's so that everyone can't get in.

Adult utterances during involvement with activities could broadly be seen to perform three functions: responding to the children; directing behaviour; giving and requesting information. (Actual examples of these are given in Appendix E, Table 2.) *Responding to the children* includes general social remarks; encouragement, discouragement; and affirming, correcting and extending a child's statement. *Directing behaviour* includes making positive or negative control statements; setting a goal; and giving directions or a demonstration. *Giving and requesting information* includes information-giving statements and information-seeking questions.

An analysis of 20 speech samples showed that the largest category of adult utterances was that concerned with information, there being slightly more information-seeking questions than information-giving statements. Directing behaviour made up the smallest group, with only a minimal number (three) of negative control remarks. Similarly, responding to children's statements included only three discouragements.

The utterances of 10 teachers and 10 assistants grouped as follows:

		Teachers		*Assistants*
Giving information	74)		72)	
Requesting information	82)	156	75)	147
Responding to the children		90		83
Directing behaviour		50		66
Total:		296		296

It will be noted that, while the teachers scored higher on 'information' and 'responding' statements, the assistants exceeded them on 'directing' statements, though in all cases the differences were small.

Within both groups there were marked differences in style. Some staff made a large proportion of information-giving statements, whilst others were more concerned with directing the children through an activity. Others used a combination of information statements and responses to children.

The 20 speech sequences were analysed in terms of four types of adult utterance: responding to the children; directing behaviour; information-giving; and information-seeking. Eight styles emerged, based on the predominance (i.e. more than 25 per cent) of certain types of utterances in each sequence. The styles were as follows:

Style	Teachers	Assistants
Directing	1	2
Information-giving	–	1
Information-giving and directing	2	–
Information-giving and responding	4	2
Information-seeking	1	–
Information-seeking and directing	–	1
Information-seeking and responding	2	3
Consistent (across all types of statements)	–	–
TOTAL	10	10

It is important to note that five of the 10 matched pairs of staff shared the same style, implying the influence which a teacher and an assistant working together may have upon each other.

Extracts from the sample showing examples of these styles are given below.

Extracts showing examples of different styles

1. *Direction*

   Adult   Turn it round. Now press harder. Now pull the pastry from round the sides. Leave your mould on. That's it.

2. *Information-giving*

   Adult   That's where it's joined on, I think. Look at those beautiful bubbles there. Can you see them in the corner? If you take that off it won't pump any more. That stops the air coming through.

3. *Information-giving and directing*

   Adult   That's right. Fill it right up. You need to push it out like this because it snags on there and it won't fill. It's going down very slowly, but it's going down, look. That's because you haven't got a hole to let the air out.

4. *Information-giving and responding*

   Child   And we've seen the Queen's castle.

Adult   At Windsor? Yes, she stays in Windsor Castle sometimes, doesn't she? Let me get my picture of Buckingham Palace to show you if the flag's flying. It means the Queen's staying in the Palace when the flag flies.

5.   *Information-seeking*

Adult   What do you have to put in tea? Do you just pour it out of a teapot or do you put anything else with it?

Child   Tea.

Adult   What do we have to put with tea usually Arlette? What else in the cup?

Child   Sugar.

6.   *Information-seeking and directing*

Adult   What colour paper would you like, boys? White or grey?

Child   White.

Adult   The only thing about the white is that it's a little bit smaller, so you mustn't put too much paint on. . . . Not very much paint or it will all run off the edge.

7.   *Information-seeking and responding*

Child   I've made a big crane.

Adult   Have you? Does it work?

Child   Yes.

Adult   What can you lift up with it?

Child   All them.

Adult   Do you? And when you lift them up where do you put them?

Child   In the lorry.

Adult   In the lorry? So you load you lorry up with your crane do you?

Child   Yes. Some lorries are so big it could break the crane.

8.   *Consistent*

Adult   What is it Rachel? Can you tell us what it is?

Child   A cooker.

Adult   A cooker, yes. Christopher, would you like a turn?

Child   I got the bike.

Adult   Pardon? Trolley. It's a toy trolley. And I've got some carrots being chopped up.

3. Complexity of adult utterances

The four types of utterances described above (i.e. responding to children, directing behaviour, giving information, requesting information) may be analysed in terms of their complexity. A system for categorizing the speech of staff within children's activities was developed for this study adapted from category systems used by Barbara Tizard[1,2] and Joan Tough[3].

(For a description of the system, see Appendix E, Table 2).

An extract from a speech sequence to which this adapted system was applied is given below. The teacher is working with a small group on a collage of the Queen.

Child	Teacher, I'm going to cut the Queen's face out.	
Adult	That's very difficult to cut right round the Queen's face, isn't it?	E
Child	Yes, 'cos the Queen looks . . .	
Adult	She looks very kind, doesn't she?	R
	Do you think she'll be pleased when she sees that picture, do you?	SH
	Have you seen the Queen visiting lots of different places?	SP
	It would be lovely if she came here, wouldn't it?	GH
	Have you seen her visiting different towns, Paul?	SP
Child	No, I haven't.	
Adult	She's in Scotland, isn't she, at the moment?	GP
	I've seen the pictures on the television.	GP
Child	She lives in London.	
Adult	At Buckingham Palace, doesn't she?	E
Child	And I've been to London to the airport.	
Adult	Have you?	Y
	Have you seen my picture of London airport over there on the wall?	E
	And of Buckingham Palace?	E
Child	And we've seen the Queen's castle.	
Adult	Windsor?	R
	Yes, she stays in Windsor Castle sometimes, doesn't she?	E
	Was the Queen staying there when you went there?	SP
Child	We just went to London and then we came back.	

Adult	Let me get my picture of Buckingham Palace to show you if the flag's flying.	GR
	Lucy, would you like to choose a picture of the Queen?	G
	I'll go and get my picture of Buckingham Palace.	GR
	Where's she going there?	SL
Child	She's going to get married.	

Every adult utterance in the 20 speech sequences was coded, and the results were as follows:

Responding to children	Teachers	Assistants
Makes general social remark	18	14
Makes positive affective remark	20	20
Makes negative affective remark	2	0
Affirms child's statement	21	24
Negates child's statement	0	0
Corrects, reinforces, makes simple extension of child utterance	18	19
Makes complex extension of child utterance	11	5
Summarizes discussion/resumé	0	1
TOTAL	90	83

Directing behaviour		
Makes positive control remark	1	0
Makes negative control remark	2	0
Sets goal	6	5
Gives simple directions/ demonstration	24	38
Gives complex directions	17	23
TOTAL	50	66

Giving information		
Gives simple indentification	3	12
Gives simple description	15	18
Gives simple comparison/relation	16	14
Gives process report/description	17	13
Gives projection outside situation	7	1
Gives logical reasoning	11	12
Gives hypothetical deduction	5	2
TOTAL	74	72

Requesting information

Requests quick decision (yes/no)	18	13
Requests simple identification	6	12
Requests simple description	1	1
Requests simple comparison/relation	21	20
Requests process report/description	10	7
Requests projection outside situation	21	21
Requests logical reasoning	4	1
Requests hypothetical deduction	1	0
TOTAL	82	75

Whilst one must be wary of making generalizations from such a small sample, several points are worth noting, and the differences between teachers and assistants discussed above can now be looked at in more detail.

1. Responding statements

It has been noted that the teachers scored slightly more on these than the assistants. The difference consisted mainly in a higher number of general social remarks and in complex extensions of child utterances. The two groups were very similar on all other categories of responding statements. (Note the minimal number of negative affective remarks).

2. Directing statements

The nursery assistants made more of this type of statement, and the analysis shows that the difference lay mainly in the number of directions they gave, both simple and complex, but most markedly simple directions. This may relate to the finding that most of the assistants used an activity as an end, focusing the attention of the children upon the skills of carrying out a specific process or series of processes.

The very small number of control remarks in the sample is worth noting.

3. Information statements

While the totals for each group are similar, the analysis revealed differences between the teachers and assistants in the use of certain categories of information-giving statements. Assistants scored higher on simple identification and simple description, while the teachers exceeded them in most of the other categories, especially projection outside the situation. This supports the finding that most of the teachers used an activity for extending the attention of the children beyond the immediate situation.

4. Information questions

Both groups of staff used more questions than information statements, but the teachers notably more. Information-seeking questions are of two kinds: those which are genuine, i.e. wanting to know the answer, and those which are used as strategies to encourage the children to think for themselves. 'Genuine' questions within an activity tended to be of the most simple kind (requesting quick decision), e.g. 'Do you want some glue?', 'Have you got a piece of paper?', 'Can you see?'. Both groups used a high proportion of these, especially the teachers. The assistants made more requests for simple identification. On all other categories differences between the groups were small or non-existent, notably on requesting projection, though teachers were slightly in the lead on all the other more complex utterances. Again, this lends some support to the differences in use of activities, though the small size of the sample renders it little more than a series of interesting case studies.

This is an area where research of a larger scale might well provide further useful insights into the diversity of speech styles used in the nursery and the variety of uses to which nursery activities may be put, as well as confirming or denying the tentative conclusions drawn here.

Chapter 10
Team-work in the Nursery

The deployment of the two professions in the nursery cannot adequately be depicted simply by describing what each did in isolation. Furthermore, although they obviously predominate, teachers and nursery assistants are not the only adults found working in nurseries. The presence, temporarily and permanently, of a variety of other adults – students, ancillaries, parents – is bound to affect the nature of team-work.

In order to collect data on adult interaction, another observation system, Method 1 (ARD:1, Appendix A) was devised. It involved the scanning in rotation of the adults in the nursery on a two-minute cycle. The dominant activity of each during the previous 30 seconds was recorded before turning to the next. Provision was made in this way for the repeated observation of up to four adults in turn. A minimum of one hour 40 minutes of such recordings was made for each half-day session. Two such sessions (am, pm) were recorded for each nursery team. (Detailed instructions for using this method, ARD:1, are given in Appendix A.) At an individual level, for teachers and assistants, the information given by this system of observation overlaps to some extent with that from Method 2, which described their task in terms of the average proportion of each session spent in the various activities (duration) and the average length of time spent in each activity before being interrupted (episode).

Method 1, using a time sampling (non-continuous) system of recording, could not give information about durations of activity, nor about who initiated any changes. It simply recorded what each adult had *mainly* been doing during the previous 30 seconds, every two minutes. It was thus possible at the end of the session only to sum up *how often* during that session each adult had been observed doing this or that, and with whom, and to sum up at the end of the study how often all adults of each type had been observed involved in the various categories of activity, and with whom.

'How often' adults were observed to be involved in this and that is obviously a function of 'overall duration' and 'episode duration', though it is likely, by reason of the way in which time sampling operates, to be a somewhat rough and ready synthesis of these inherently more precise measures.

'How often', then, is perhaps the measure which best character- izes the experience of the different adults during the nursery session, at a 'coarse-grained' level. How coarse-grained it is de- pends on the appropriateness of the 30-second unit of time used. Reference to the tables of average duration of involvement (Chapter 7, page 52) suggests that it was very well-chosen: it coincides with the shortest. (This does not mean, of course, that there will necessarily be complete agreement between 'duration', 'episode', and 'how often' in any particular instance, but they are likely to agree in general.)

Team composition varied between nurseries, and for some nurseries between sessions. The total number of staff included in each set of observations varied accordingly. In order to make fair comparisons across the groups, average frequencies (of activity and context) were calculated, then standardized (adjusted) to take account of different session length. The activities and context were categorized at a more general level than for Method 2. The category and context system is presented in full in Appendix A.

Detailed tables reporting on average how often and with whom the different adults were observed to be involved are included as Appendix F, Tables 1 to 4.

The table on p.83 summarizes 'how often' in rank order of categories of activities. (For details of the categories see Appendix A.)

The two columns marked with the asterisks make a direct comparison between teachers and assistants analogous to the com- parisons made throughout Chapter 8. Table 5, Appendix F lists the activities for which there were *statistically significant* differences between how often teachers and assistants were observed to be involved in the different categories of activity. These are now

Head	Teachers in Charge	Other Teachers	All Teachers*	Nursery Assistants*	NNEB Students	Parents etc.	All Staff
Resp.	Resp.	Resp.	Resp.	Resp.	Resp.	Resp.	Resp.
Ad. talk	Superv.	Superv.	Superv.	House	House	Equip.	Superv.
Superv.	Equip.	Equip.	Equip.	Equip.	Equip.	House	Equip.
Admin.	Ad. talk	Ad. talk	Ad. talk	Superv.	Superv.	Superv.	House
Equip.	Garden	Garden	Garden	Garden	Supp.	Welfare	Garden
Welfare	Welfare	House	Welfare	Welfare	Garden	Ad. talk	Welfare
Conv.	Conv.	Welfare	Conv.	Ad. talk	Welfare	Garden	Ad. talk
House	House	Conv.	House	Supp.	Ad. talk	Conv.	Conv.
Supp.	Admin.	Admin.	Admin.	Conv.	Conv.	Supp.	Supp.
Garden	Supp.	Supp.	Supp.	Admin.	Admin.	Admin.	Admin.

briefly discussed.

When they were working independently of other adults, teachers were observed more often to be involved in responsibility, supervision, adult talk and administration – with large groups of children and with parents or other visitors. When assistants were working independently of other adults they were observed more often to be involved with housework, organization of equipment, and welfare.

When they were working as a team, the teachers were observed more often to be involved with responsibility, supervision, social conversation and welfare – in fact, contacts with children generally – whereas assistants were more often observed to be involved with housework, the organization of equipment and administration, working not in contact with children.

Thus for staff, whether working alone or in a team, involvement in children's activities predominated, with assistants tending to provide support by dealing with the upkeep of the physical environment. This agrees closely with the findings reported in Chapter 8, as might well have been expected.

Turning to differences amongst teachers when working independently, head teachers were observed more often to be involved in administration and adult talk than teachers-in-charge, but vice versa for supervision, thus reflecting the wider-ranging authority (over a whole school) of the head teacher, and the relatively 'class-bound' role of the teacher-in-charge. In fact, teachers-in-charge were observed more often to be involved in supervision than class teachers. Head teachers were more often observed to be involved with individual children and with parents and visitors than were class teachers or teachers-in-charge. Class teachers were more often observed to be involved with nursery assistants than either of the other types of teachers.

When working in a team, teachers-in-charge were more often observed to be involved in supervision, social conversation and welfare, than class teachers, who in turn were more often observed to be involved in housework, organization of equipment and administration than teachers-in-charge.

To sum up, head teachers tended to be involved in contact with adults; teachers-in-charge, with children. Head teachers tended to make the most contacts with individual children, which is entirely logical. Such contacts were rarely a part of the on-going fabric of the session, but were more usually *ad hoc* in nature, whereas the involvement of other teachers with children was generally part of the planned daily routine. There were some instances of talk between teachers and assistants but *in the main talk between staff was minimal.* Of the few instances of talk engaged in by NNEB students and parent-helpers, a greater number were with assistants than other staff. With this brief introduction to team-work in the nursery, it is appropriate now to have a look at patterns of staff deployment.

Team size and composition varied between nurseries and sometimes between sessions:

4-member teams	*No. in Study*
1. Teacher-in-charge; 2nd teacher; 2 nursery assistants	4
2. Teacher-in-charge; 2nd teacher; nursery assistant; 1 parent or other helper	2
3. Head teacher; 2nd teacher; 2 nursery assistants	2
4. Teacher-in-charge; 3 nursery assistants ..	2
5. Teacher-in-charge; 2 nursery assistants; 1 student NNEB	2
6. Class teacher; 2 nursery assistants; 1 student NNEB	2
	14

3-member teams	
1. Teacher-in-charge; 1 nursery assistant; 1 student NNEB	17
2. Class teacher; 1 nursery assistant; 1 student NNEB	6
3. Head teacher; 2 nursery assistants	4
4. Teacher-in-charge; 2 nursery assistants ..	3
5. Class teacher; 1 nursery assistant; 1 parent or other helper	1
	31

2-member teams

1. Teacher-in-charge; 1 nursery assistant ...   30
2. Class teacher; 1 nursery assistant   3
3. Head teacher; 1 nursery assistant   2
                                                       ——
                                                       35

TOTAL . . . = 80 (Sessions)

Team composition may best be appreciated in relation to team size:

Team Size	Adult + 1	Adult + 2		Adult + 3		Adult 4
2-member teams	Teacher +	Nursery assistant				
3-member teams	Teacher +	Nursery assistant	+ either or or	Nursery assistant NNEB Student Parent/ helper		
4-member teams	Teacher + or	2nd teacher Nursery assistant	+	Nursery assistant either or or	+	Nursery assistant Student NNEB Parent/ helper

In attempting to look at patterns of deployment across teams of different size and composition, comparison by session is confounded by the normal coming and goings of staff in the nursery. For example during the 10-minute coffee break of two members of staff, an original team of four would be operating as a team of two, and when a head teacher is called away to deal with a matter in another part of the building, the only other member of staff working in the room would be left to cope single-handed.

It therefore seemed preferable to look at recurring patterns of deployment within each two-minute observation in which four, three or two members of staff might be working alongside each other as well as observing the activities engaged in by staff working on their own. This strategy allowed for comparisons to be made between recurring patterns in respect of the activities going on, distinguishing between those involving the children, and those associated with nursery organization.

This table depicts the comparison between the most prevalent pattern of deployment of two-member teams, and four member teams:

Staff members	2-member teams		4-member teams			
	1	2	1	2	3	4
Pattern of deployment:						
Contributory activities	R3 (Resp. for large gp)	H (H'work)	R3 (Resp. for large gp)	U (Support. in large gp)	H (H'work)	H (H'work)
whether A - to do with children or B - to do with organization	A	B	A	A	B	B
Proportionate representation	A = 50%	B = 50%	A = 50%		B = 50%	

As might be expected, the patterns of deployment recurred more frequently in small teams than large, purely as a function of more limited possibilities. The 10 most prevalent patterns of deployment for the different sized teams (4,3,2 and 1 adult working alone) are presented as Table 6, Appendix F.

Deployment in most teams (irrespective of size) involved different staff in children's activities on the one hand, and tasks such as housework and the organization of equipment on the other. It is intersting that in the most frequently occurring patterns of both four-member and two-member teams, deployment was between *complementary* activities (i.e. 'involvement' in children's activities and 'housework'), whereas for three-member teams it was in *parallel* activities (mainly 'responsibility'). However, to make a comparison of 'parallel' and 'complementary' types of deployment across teams of different size is difficult owing to the wide variety of possible combinations of staff within the division of activities.

Responsibility for children's activities plus housework plus organization of equipment are the activities that feature most often in two-, three- and four-member teams with, not surprisingly, more instances of activities relating to supervision than responsibility featuring among the activities of a single member of staff working alone (Table 7, Appendix F).

Activities directly associated with children predominate in teams of whatever size (Table 8, Appendix F).

The variation in the number of adults making up the nursery team has already been described. The team in any one nursery fluctuated from day to day, session to session, and even within a session. Teams varied in the numbers of teachers and assistants they contained. Many nurseries also made use of other working adults, such as students, parents, and pupils from local secondary schools. The presence of a working adult was not always constant throughout a session: a mother might help out for an hour or so, and the 'permanent' staff might leave the nursery for breaks, outings with a group of children, staff meetings, or duties elsewhere in the school. Students and secondary school helpers might be present only on certain days, and some permanent staff might be part-time.

The most common situation observed, however, was *two* adults working with 11 to 20 children, and the next most common was the same number of children with three adults (the third often being an NNEB student). Other combinations occurred mostly in atypical situations, such as coffee breaks, and preparation for and clearing up from sessions, though these situations did not usually last for long.

It was felt to be important to see how the kind of work done by the 80 staff was related to the numbers of working adults present. Three groups were considered: teachers, assistants and others. The data were obtained by Method 2 (Chapter 7).

The relationship was investigated between the number of *teachers* in the area of observation and the durations and frequencies of summary categories of tasks for the staff being observed. The number of teachers present ranged from nought to three. Behaviours which significantly *increased* with more teachers present were:

Administration	:	(duration)
Adult talk	:	(duration and frequency)
Involvement	:	(frequency)
Self-initiations	:	(frequency)

Other-initiations	:	(duration and frequency)
Working with individual children	:	(duration and frequency)

Behaviours which significantly *decreased* with more teachers present were:

Supervision	:	(duration)
Self-initiations	:	(duration)
Working alone	:	(duration)

Certain behaviours were observed most when there was only *one* teacher present:

Involvement	:	(duration) though this increased again when there were three teachers present
Working with children	:	(duration)
Working with small groups	:	(duration)

Things which varied most with the number of teachers present were administration, adult talk, supervision and involvement. These are all behaviours which tend to fall more into the domain of teachers. On the other hand, housework and equipment, which tended towards the assistant's domain, remained unaffected.

A similar exercise was carried out on the relationship between the number of nursery *assistants* present and observed behaviour. Behaviours which significantly *increased* with more assistants present were:

Housework	:	(duration)
Adult talk	:	(duration and frequency)
Working with individual children	:	(frequency)
Working with small groups	:	(duration)
Working with children	:	(duration) though the last two fell again when there were more than two assistants present.

Behaviours which *decreased* with more assistants present were:

Working alone	:	(duration)

Working with adults   (frequency)
                                       though this increased again
                                       with three assistants present.

There were some interesting variations. Far more administration
was done when there were *no* assistants present than when there
were some, reinforcing the view that the teachers did most of the
administrative tasks, often working at them alone. Two areas of
behaviour, active and passive supervision, were observed more
when there were *three* assistants present than with any fewer.
Where only *one* assistant was present, most involvement but least
working with individuals were observed.

'Others' included students, ancillaries, parent helpers and secondary school pupils. The number noted in any one nursery at one
time ranged from nought to four. Behaviours which significantly
increased with the number of other adults present were:

Other-initiation   :   (duration)
Working with children   :   (duration)
Working with individuals   :   (duration and frequency)
Adult talk   :   (duration and frequency)
                                   though the last two fell when
                                   three other adults were
                                   present.

Behaviours which *decreased* when more other adults were present
were:

Supervision   :   (duration and frequency)
Welfare   :   (duration and frequency)
Working alone   :   (duration)
Working with adults   :   (duration and frequency)

Most involvement was observed when there were *three* others
present, suggesting that this is the optimum number for facilitating
maximum participation by the permanent staff in the children's
activities. The number of others present bore no significant relationship with the amount of housework, dealing with equipment,
administration, conversation or passive supervision carried out by
the 80 staff.

The evidence thus suggests that the quality of work in the nursery
is critically affected by the number and type of adults present in the
team at any time. Almost all observed behaviours were affected.

Only working with large groups showed no significant differences, suggesting that the more formal activities like story and music time were carried out irrespective of team size.

The evidence suggests that a greater number of adults working in the nursery leads to more adult talk, more other-initiated behaviours and less working alone. It also means that less time was spent by the 'permanent' staff on supervisory tasks. However, that most important part of the nursery programme, involvement in children's activities, does not necessarily increase with team size. Observations suggested that involvement increased with the number of teachers, but reached a maximum when not more than two assistants or not more than three other working adults were present. This supports the view expressed by many staff that there can be *too many* helpers, particularly in a small nursery.

Whilst in some nurseries differences in responsibilities (ascribed and perceived) between the two professions were very clear-cut, in others they definitely were not. This variety was subsumed in the averages on the basis of which role differentiation was reported in Chapter 6.

It was of considerable interest, therefore, to see whether the deployment of staff varied according to *how* differentiated their role was: were they deployed along clear-cut professional lines when there were clear-cut differences in their responsibilities, and were they deployed irrespective of profession when their responsibilities were seen as being very similar?

From the number of exclusive or shared responsibilities, the differentiation between teachers' and nursery assistants' working role was derived. Details of the derivation of a 'role differentiation score' for each nursery are given in Appendix F.

This score was used to allocate each nursery to one of four levels of staff role differentiation: high; moderately high; moderately low; and low (Tables 9 and 10). The data on duration of activity and frequency of involvement in activities from Method 2 (ARD:2) were then reanalysed to see whether staff deployment reflected these different degrees of role differentiation. A multivariate analysis of variance was used for this purpose (MANOVA*).

---

* SPSS: MANOVA: Multivariate Analysis of Variance and Covariance. Document N.413. COHEN, E. and BURNS, P. North-Western University, Vogelback Computing Centre, Illinois.

Differences between teachers and assistants irrespective of role differentiation abound (Appendix F, Tables 12 - 2b, 14 - 2b), but since they have been discussed exhaustively in Chapter 8, they are merely acknowledged here.

There was only the slightest evidence in these analyses (Tables 11, 12, 13, 14) that differences in role differentiation as measured by ascribed responsibilities were reflected in differences in the way that staff were deployed.

Differences between mean frequencies of involvement of staff in the nine summary activities came just short of being statistically significant at the five per cent level in combination (Table 12 -2a). Taken separately, differences in involvement in children's activities, housework and adult talk reached statistical significance, in that order of importance. Inspection of the means (Table 11) indicates that as role differentiation decreases, teachers became *less* often involved with children, *more* often involved in talking with other adults, and *more* often involved with housework. Trends amongst the means for assistants are less marked, the only one really of note being a slight decrease in housework with a decline in role differentiation.

Differences between mean durations of involvement of staff in the nine summary activities again came just short of being statistically significant at the five per cent level in combination (Table 14 - 2a). Taken separately, the difference between means for equipment was the only one to reach statistical significance, both teachers and assistants tending to be involved in this activity for longer in nurseries where role differentiation was less (Table 13).

It will be recalled that there was general agreement amongst staff concerning their ascribed and perceived responsibilities (Chapter 6). This should be borne in mind when considering the significance of the very modest influence of high and low role differentiation in staff deployment. In fact, in so far as deployment was influenced by low role differentiation, it was in rather undesirable ways, with teachers doing more of the 'domestic' work at the expense of less 'educational' involvement in children's activities. However, these trends were very slight compared with the overwhelming influence of traditional roles. Training and tradition thus seemed to be the most powerful determinants of the nursery day for the two professions, relatively unaffected by local agreements to see things differently.

There was, however, one notable exception to this general conclusion. It was observed that the nursery teacher, rather than the assistant, invariably carried the overall responsibility for the class or group of children. But if for any reason the teacher was not present (having left the room to carry out some administrative task, take a group of children elsewhere, supervise in the garden etc.) the assistant would then briefly assume responsibility. In order to see what effect, if any, this assumption of responsibility had on staff behaviour, a sheet-by-sheet record was kept (Method II: of each 15-minute period, 1,600 sheets in all) of whether the person observed was 'responsible' or 'not responsible', and the data analysed accordingly.

When she was 'responsible' ('in charge'), the member of staff did significantly more administration and involvement in children's activities, less housework and organization of equipment. She worked more with the children, especially with small groups, and less by herself. She engaged more in activities initiated by others (that is, was more responsive to children's overt needs). None of the other categories of staff behaviour was affected.

Being 'responsible' thus led assistants to behave in ways which were characteristic of teachers (see Chapter 8): they became 'acting teachers'.

An interesting parallel is reported by Tizard* in respect of trained and untrained staff in residential day nurseries: 'When "in charge", the behaviour of trained and untrained staff could not be distinguished.' (page 357.) Both illustrate the power of implicit role ascription.

It must of course be borne in mind that whilst these conclusions about the effect of role on behaviour are valid at the general level, they will not necessarily hold true at the individual level, where such matters as staff age and temperament (which tend to randomize out at the general level) hold sway.

Reference*

TIZARD, B. *et al.* (1972). 'Environmental effects on language development: a study of young children in long-stay residential nurseries', *Child Dev.*, **43** 337-58.

Chapter 11

Summing Up

To what extent, then, do the training and tradition, the aims and perceived responsibilities of the two professions influence the way they behave, and are there '. . . clear advantages to the employment of nursery teachers *rather than* nursery nurses?'

The teachers generally seemed to feel that their initial training had shortcomings of a more or less serious kind, whereas the assistants were generally satisfied with theirs. However, negative views about their own status were expressed by both the teachers *vis-à-vis* their colleagues in the primary schools, to which many of the nurseries were attached, and the assistants in relation to the limited career opportunities which possession of the NNEB Certificate afforded in the education sector. Each had professional links beyond the nursery – the teachers with other sectors of education (three quarters had worked with older children at sometime in their careers); the assistants with Social Services (all but one had worked in such settings, approximately half of them in day nurseries and hospitals).

There was general agreement between the aims of the staff in this study and those of the much larger number (of teachers only) in the Taylor study (op.cit.). Teachers and assistants both volunteered 'social' aims the most frequently and 'linguistic' aims the least. They differed mainly in the frequency with which they expressed educational aims, the teachers volunteering these more often than the assistants.

Staff role was defined as the responsibilities which were ascribed to staff by their superiors and the responsibilities which they perceived to be theirs. There was broad agreement between ascribed and perceived responsibilities, which seemed to coalesce into eight areas of function. Administration of the nursery, planning of the programme, involvement in children's activities, and talk with other adults were seen primarily as the responsibility of teachers. Assistants were seen as being primarily responsible for welfare and housework. Responsibility for the supervision of children and the organization of equipment was shared more or less equally. There was overall agreement on this division of responsibility in all three types of nursery, but there was, of course, considerable variation in how clearly *differentiated* were the responsibilities of teachers and assistants. Where role differentiation was low, the teachers tended, as might be expected, to be more often involved in the domestic work of the nursery at the expense of their involvement with the children, which did not seem to be compensated for by a commensurate increase in such involvement on the part of assistants. It would appear that moves towards egalitarianism in the nursery are not to the children's advantage.

Turning to staff deployment, 60 per cent of staff time was spent working with children, either supervising them or involving them in various activities. Twenty per cent of staff time was spent in 'social contacts' – in conversation with children, and in conversation with the various other adults present. The remaining twenty per cent of the nursery day was occupied in physically maintaining the nursery – in administration, housework, and the organization of the equipment.

Changes in staff task were very frequent – on average 175 every session, almost one a minute. About four fifths of these changes seemed to occur as a result of staff decision rather than as a result of the direct demand of others.

In respect of all three measures of activity – overall duration, frequency of change, and average duration of episodes of activity – teachers and assistants were clearly differentiated. But the activities which contributed to differentiation were the *domestic* ones: housework, administration, and organization of equipment. Those activities which included direct contact with children, particularly involvement in children's activities, made a weak or negligible contribution to differential deployment.

In the light of the way in which aims and roles appeared to be differentiated, that teachers and assistants should be differentiated by domestic activities was entirely to be expected. But that the 'educational' activity should not differentiate was not expected, and the possibility was considered that this was an artefact of the composite nature of the 'educational' category, 'involvement in children's activities', which is the aggregate of 24 more specific activities. When staff were compared for each, however, it was only in respect of five – books, primary school skills, wheeled toys and apparatus, investigation, and stories – that there were any differences which reached statistical significance. Even for these, there were no significant differences in the average durations of episodes. It was only in respect of overall duration of investigation, and stories that teachers and assistants were *substantially* differentiated.

It was when the language used by teachers and assistants in the context of this summary category of activity was studied that differentiation between the professions, consistent with expectations, perhaps occurred. It is necessary to be somewhat tentative because the differences were qualitative and had not been obtained in such a way as to be evaluated statistically.

Differentiation between teachers and assistants seemed to be of three kinds: the *use* of the activity being made by the adult, as inferred from the speech used; the *style* of discourse employed; and the *complexity* of the speech.

With regard to use, the evidence suggested that teachers tended to use activities as means to ends, and assistants as ends in themselves. The differences in style of speech were relatively insignificant, teachers emphasizing 'informative' and 'responsive' statements, and the assistants, 'directing' statements. Regarding complexity, there was evidence in the transcripts of a tendency for teachers to make complex extensions to children's utterances. Assistants tended to make more 'directing' statements, and generally these were markedly simple in structure. Teachers made more use of 'projection' when giving and seeking information, in contrast to assistants who made more use of simple 'identification' and 'description' statements.

The most common size of nursery team in the study was two – a teacher and an assistant. The least common was four. Two- and four- member teams were most often deployed between *complementary* activities (i.e. involvement in children's activities for the teacher(s), housework for the assistant(s).) Three-member teams were most often observed to be deployed between parallel activities (i.e. all three sharing 'responsibility'). The more teachers there were, the greater the quantity of administration, adult talk, and other-initiations, the less supervision. The more assistants there were, the greater the quantity of housework, adult talk, and working with small groups of children. The more other adults there were, the more other-initiation, working with children, working with individual children, and adult talk. Most involvement in children's activities was observed when there were three other adults present. It decreased when more were there, suggesting that this is the 'educationally optimum' number and that there can be 'too many' helpers, particularly in a small nursery.

The picture which emerges from this study is of two professions, each with its distinctive training and tradition, each with its beliefs about what it is aiming to do and what its specific responsibilities are, working side-by-side in the nursery. The assistants are deployed to maintain the environment; the teachers to administer it, planning its activities, and in overall charge. To this extent the behaviour of the two professions is consistent with expectations. When the 'educational' interaction between adults and children is considered, the evidence of differentiation along expected lines is equivocal, and it is far from certain that there are advantages for the children when a teacher rather than her assistant is involved in nursery activities with them.

It has been suggested, both by educationists (e.g. Parry and Archer, op.cit.) and practitioners (e.g. Robinson and Banbury, op.cit.) that the distinctive feature of the nursery teacher is that she is a *team leader*. The evidence from this study suggests that the teachers involved generally saw themselves that way (aims and responsibilities) and behaved that way (in the hierarchy of activities). Here then is a possible answer to the question posed. If nursery education is characterized by team-work, then there is a clear need for both leaders and led. No good purpose would be served by employing either to the exclusion of the other.

Appendix A: Instruments

Aims, Role and Deployment of Staff in the Nursery
Final List of methods used

Method I

	Activity		Context
H	Housework	0	Self
E	Equipment	1	Individual
A	Administration	2	Small group
T	Adult talk	3	Large group
S	Supervision	4	Head
C	Conversation	5	Teacher
W	Welfare	6	Assistant
U	Supportive	7	Student
R	Responsible	8	Other working adults
G	Garden	9	Parents & visitors
L	Going out	*	Staff group

Method II

	Activity		Context
H	Housework	0	Self
E	Equipment	1	Individual
A	Administration	2	Small group
S	Active supervision	(12	Small group)
PS	Passive supervision		(individually)
C	Conversation	(82	Small group)
W	Welfare		(supportive)
		3	Large group
	Adult talk	(13	Large group)
AT	Admin.		(individually)
ET	Equip.	(83	Large group)
ST	Superv.		(supportive)
HT	Housework	4	Head
WT	Welfare	5	Teacher
DT	Develop.	6	Assistant
RT	Org. staff		
CT	Social con.		**Students:**
		57	Teaching
	Resp. Activity	67	Assistants (NNEB)
X	Books, pictures	8	Ancillaries

Method II *contd.*

K	Playcorner	9	Parents
UK	Musical instruments	(89	Working parents)
N	Sand etc.	(79	Other vol. helpers,
R	Water		sec. sch. ch.)
G	Clay, plasticine etc.	(99	Visitors)
WW	Woodwork	56	Staff group
Q	Art/Craft	26	Children/staff group
	(DQ-Colouring/	19	Children/parents
	drawing, PQ-Painting/		group
	printing, CQ-Collage,	18	Child from primary
	cutting etc., JQ-Junk		school
	modelling etc.)	58	Staff from primary
T	Floor toys (train, car		school
	layouts)	P =	used as a suffix when
Z	Puzzles		X,Z etc. are used as a
P	Primary skills		medium for primary
B	Construction (lego,		school skills
	mechano)	>	self-initiated
J	Wheeled toys/	<	other-initiated
	apparatus		
I	Investigation		
Y	Stories/rhymes		
D	Drama		
PC	Prayers		
U	Music		
V	TV/vis. speakers		
M	Milk time		
CF	Cooking		
PF	Party		

ARD:1
Guidelines for administering ARD observation: Method I

Introduction

The system is designed to provide a description of the division of work amongst all the staff in the nursery classroom, during the course of a day. The staff are scanned on a cyclical basis, the behaviour of each being observed and coded for 30 seconds, each two-minute interval.

The category system

The dominant behaviour during 30 seconds is coded on two dimensions: 'Activity' and 'Context'. The categories and codes are as follows:–

	Activity		Context
H	Housework	0	Self
E	Equipment	1	Individual
A	Administration	2	Small group
T	Adult talk	3	Large group
S	Supervision	4	Head
C	Conversation	5	Teacher
W	Welfare	6	Assistant
U	Supportive	7	Student
R	Responsible	8	Other working adults
G	Garden	9	Parents & visitors
L	Going out	*	Staff group

Definitions of each category and examples are given below.

Completing the observation schedules

Each schedule codes the behaviour of up to four staff for 20 minutes. These schedules should be completed continuously throughout each half day session, allowing no more than five minutes break between schedules. A minimum of five schedules should normally be completed each half day session, a total of one hour 40 minutes observation time.

Use of the optical scanning sheets

The schedules have been especially printed for fast machine reading. The machine reads the presence or absence of a pencil mark within the tiny boxes over which the letters are printed. The machine is only sensitive to ordinary lead pencil. Do not use any other marking method. Mark one activity and one context code each 30 seconds by making a small clear vertical line through the appropriate letter. Do not mark the boxes anywhere else. If a mistake is made, do not try to delete it. Lightly pencil the correct code alongside the appropriate box. The schedule will be corrected later.

Selection of staff

Include all staff, up to four, in the schedules. Use the same staff for all the schedules. If there are more than four adults working in the nursery, include all permanent staff, and any others as space is available, including students, and working parents.

Definition of categories

ACTIVITY CATEGORIES

H – HOUSEWORK: i.e. moving furniture, setting tables for lunch, sweeping, mopping, cleaning, washing-up, preparing food and milk for children, making tea and coffee etc.

E – ORGANISATION OF EQUIPMENT: i.e. preparing, setting-out and replenishing materials for children's activities; clearing-up equipment; drying, writing names on and displaying paintings, collage work etc. (Includes all organization of equipment which takes place outside the context of children's on-going activity. Where organization of equipment is incidental to adult's involvement in children's on-going activity, code as R – see below).

A – ADMINISTRATION: i.e. marking register, answering telephone, checking numbers for milk, dealing with routine matters, office work etc.

T – ADULT TALK: i.e. conversation with adults in the nursery, including other staff, students, parents, visitors and other helpers.

S – SUPERVISION: i.e. organizing children towards various aspects of the nursery programme e.g. story-time, washing, lunch, going home; suggesting new activities, and prohibiting undesirable behaviour; arbitrating in disputes; monitoring children's activities, 'keeping an eye' on children.

C – CONVERSATION WITH CHILDREN: i.e. greeting children, general socializing, discussing children's experiences at home etc. (Includes all conversation which take place outside the context of children's on-going activity. Where conversation takes place within the context of adult's involvement in children's activity, code as R, see below).

W   – WELFARE: i.e. dressing, (including assistance with dressing-up clothes), helping children with aprons, hugging, comforting, washing children; giving First Aid; giving out food and milk. (Includes all cases where adult actually helps children. Where supervises children to some aspect of welfare, code as S.)

U   – INVOLVEMENT IN ACTIVITY/SUPPORTIVE IN GROUP: i.e. involved in children's activity but not leading the group of children. Applies particularly to story-time and other large group activities where one adult takes story, and a second supports the group.

R   – INVOLVEMENT IN ACTIVITY/RESPONSIBLE FOR GROUP: i.e. involved in children's activity and responsible (at that moment) for it. 'Involvement' requires that the adult works with the children in the activity, guiding them, questioning them, discussing with them, helping them progress and complete what they are doing.

U&R – Include all nursery materials, and resources; book corner, play corner, sand, water, clay, woodwork, art and craft, floor toys, puzzles, construction toys, wheeled toys and apparatus, pets, story, drama, music, TV, cooking, party etc.

G   – GARDEN: i.e. supervising children in the garden. Includes all work undertaken outside, except where normally indoor work is taken outside, e.g. painting outside on a warm day. In these cases, distinguish G – General garden duties, from R – responsible for children's activities.

L   – LEFT NURSERY: i.e. member of staff has left area of observation, for another part of school, or outside school. Continue to code L – until adult returns if at all. Also includes taking children on outings.

CONTEXT CATEGORIES

0 – SELF: i.e. adult is working by herself, not directly involving other adults or children. Where adult is having personal time, e.g coffee break, cloakroom etc., code as SO.

1 – INDIVIDUAL CHILD: i.e. adult is working with one child. Occasionally code 1 even though there is more than one child, where adult's focus of attention is predominantly with one child, e.g. child seeking welfare, brings another for comfort.

2 – SMALL and INFORMAL GROUP: i.e. working with group of approximately 2-10 children. Use this code for most informal group situations.

3 – LARGE and FORMAL GROUP: i.e. working with all or most of the nusery group. Use this code for most of the formal group times (e.g. story, music) even if the numbers may be low.

4 – HEAD TEACHER: i.e. working with or talking to the head of the school.

5 – TEACHER(S): i.e. working with or talking to a teacher or teachers.

6 – NURSERY ASSISTANT(S): i.e. working with or talking to a nursery assistant or assistants.

7 – STUDENT(S): i.e. working with or talking to a student or students, either teaching student or NNEB student.

8 – OTHER WORKING ADULTS: i.e. working with or talking to other adults, parents, voluntary helpers, secondary school pupils, who are working in the nursery.

9 – PARENTS AND VISITORS: i.e. talking to parents, particularly when delivering or collecting children. Talking to visitors at school.

* – STAFF GROUP: i.e. working with or talking to a mixed group of working adults.

Examples

ADULT 1 – working with five children on cutting and sticking – code as R2.

ADULT 2 – sorting out paper suitable for potato printing; on her own – code as E0.

ADULT 3 – Arranging next week's rota of duties with the help of a student – code as A7.

ADULT 4 – talking with a group of parents who are waiting to collect their children. Although there are children in the group, the main focus of her attention is on the parents – code as T9.

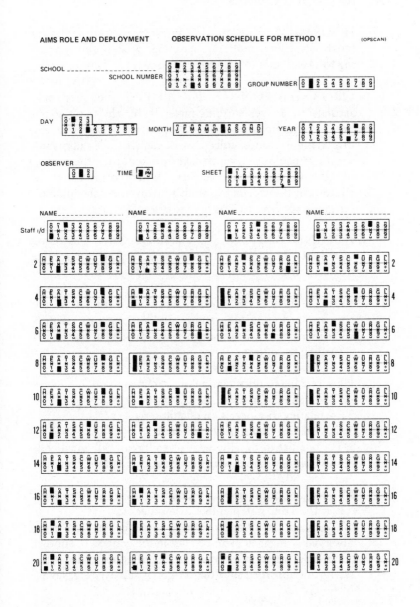

ARD:2
Expansion of Method I categories for Method II observation

ACTIVITY CATEGORIES

H – HOUSEWORK: i.e. moving furniture, setting tables for lunch, sweeping, mopping, cleaning, washing-up, preparing food and milk for children, making tea and coffee etc.

E – ORGANIZATION OF EQUIPMENT: i.e. preparing, setting-out and replenishing materials for children's activities; clearing-up equipment; drying, writing names on and displaying paintings, collage work etc. (Includes all organization of equipment which takes place outside the context of children's on-going activity. Where organization of equipment is incidental to adult's involvement in children's on-going activity, code as R – see below.)

A – ADMINISTRATION: i.e. marking register, answering telephone, checking numbers for milk, dealing with routine matters, office work etc.

T – ADULT TALK: i.e. conversation with adults in the nursery, including other staff, students, parents, visitors and other helpers. This category sub-divided at Method II according to content.
AT – relating to administration
ET – relating to organization of equipment
HT – relating to housework
ST – relating to supervision of children
WT – relating to welfare of children
DT – relating to development of children (individual children's abilities, and discussion about curriculum, activities etc).
RT – organization of staff, training of students, referrals of duties from one staff member to another etc.
CT – social conversation (Where a member of staff being observed is engaged in an activity in the context of another adult, any conversation they engage in is *not* coded separately but absorbed into the on-going activity, e.g. laying

table for lunch (housework) with NNEB student, together with related discussion, coded as H.67.)

S – SUPERVISION: i.e. organizing children towards various aspects of the nursery programme, e.g. story-time, washing, lunch, going home, suggesting new activities, and prohibiting undesirable behaviour, arbitrating in disputes, monitoring children's activities, 'keeping an eye' on children.

At Method II *Active* and *Passive* Supervision coded separately:
S – Active (actively organizing children, arbitrating etc).
PS – Passive (minimal supervision, observing but not becoming personally involved).

C – CONVERSATION WITH CHILDREN: i.e. greeting children, general socializing, discussing children's experiences at home etc. (Includes all conversation which takes place outside the context of children's on-going activity. Where conversation takes place within the context of adult's involvement in children's activity, code as R, see below.)

W – WELFARE: i.e. dressing, (including assistance with dressing-up clothes), helping children with aprons, hugging, comforting, washing children; giving First Aid; giving out food and milk – informally not as part of group activity. (Includes all cases where adult actually *helps* children. Where she *directs* children to some aspect of welfare, code as S.)

U – INVOLVEMENT IN ACTIVITY/SUPPORTIVE IN GROUP: i.e. involved in children's activity but not leading the group of children. Applies particularly to story-time and other large group activities where one adult takes story and a second supports the group. This category redundant at Method II as supportive role in an activity shown in the context code: prefix 8 before 2 (small group) or 3 (large or formal group).

R – INVOLVEMENT IN ACTIVITY/RESPONSIBLE FOR GROUP: i.e. involved in children's activity and responsible (at that moment) for it. 'Involvement' requires that the adult works with the children in the activity, guiding them, questioning them, discussing with them, helping them progress and complete what they are doing. (See also C above).

At Method II R is replaced by specific activity codes:

X – Pictures, books
K – Playcorner and imaginative play extending beyond corner
UK – Musical instruments corner
N – Sand, soil etc.
R – Water play
G – Clay, plasticine, dough, pastry
WW – Woodwork
DQ – Colouring, drawing,
PQ – Painting, printing
CQ – Collage, cutting and sticking
JQ – Junk modelling
T – Floor toys: large bricks, skittles, road and rail layouts etc.
Z – Puzzles; matching, sorting games; jigsaws, beads, sewing etc.
P – 'Primary school' skills (i.e. reading, writing and number work)
B – Construction toys, e.g. lego, mechano, small bricks etc.
J – Wheeled toys and apparatus, balls, hoops etc.
I – Investigation and discovery: animals and plants; colour and interest tables; charts, calendars etc.
Y – Stories and rhymes
D – Drama, i.e. acting-games, miming etc.
U – Music, i.e. making and listening to and using music
V – Television programmes and visiting speakers, roadsafety, child care etc.
M – Milk time when used as a specific group activity
CF – Cooking
PF – Party

G – GARDEN: i.e. supervising children in garden. Includes all work undertaken outside, except where normally indoor work is taken outside, e.g. painting outside on a warm day. In these cases, distinguish G – general garden duties, from R – responsible for children's activities.

This category not used at Method II as possible to follow member of staff into garden to continue recording her activities, a note being made of the new location.

L – LEFT NURSERY: i.e. member of staff has left area of observation, for another part of school, or outside school. Continue to code L – until adult returns if at all. Also includes taking children on outings.

At Method II possible to clarify reason for member of staff's departure and whether or not she is still a working member of the nursery.

CONTEXT CATEGORIES

0 – SELF: i.e. adult is working by herself, not directly involving other adults or children. Where adult is having personal time, e.g. coffee break, cloakroom etc., code as S0.

1 – INDIVIDUAL CHILD: i.e. adult is working with one child. Occasionally code 1 even though there is more than one child, where adult's focus of attention is predominantly with one child, e.g. child seeking welfare, brings another for comfort.

(In the supervision of individual children, only where the nature of the supervision changes from child to child is it coded as a series of S1s, e.g. supervising one child towards the garden, second child to finish drinking his milk, third child to put bricks away etc. Where the supervision of children is towards same goal or for same reason code as S12, S13, as detailed under small group/large group context codes.)

2 – SMALL and INFORMAL GROUP: i.e. working with group of approximately 2-10 children. Use this code for most informal group situations.

Possible to show member of staff's 'style' of Supervision in context code at Method II:

S2 – seeking 'whole group' attention – *collective* supervision.

S12 – organization of group through *individual* supervision.

(Also at Method II, 82 denotes supportive role in group activity.)

3 – LARGE and FORMAL GROUP: i.e. working with all or most of the nursery group. Use this code for most of the formal group times (e.g. story, music) even if the numbers may be low.

As with small group, possible to show member of staff's 'style' of Supervision in context code at Method II:

S3 – seeking 'whole group' attention '- *collective* supervision

S13 – organization of group through *individual* supervision

(Also at Method II, 83 – denotes supportive role in large and formal group activity.)

4 – HEAD TEACHER: i.e. working with or talking to the head of the school.

5 – TEACHER(S): i.e. working with or talking to a teacher or teachers.

6 – NURSERY ASSISTANT(S): i.e. working with or talking to a nursery assistant or assistants.

7 – STUDENT(S): i.e. working with or talking to a student or students, either teaching student or NNEB student.

Teaching students and NNEB students coded separately at Method II:

57 – Teaching Student

67 – NNEB Student

8 – OTHER WORKING ADULTS: i.e. working with or talking to other adults, parents, voluntary helpers, secondary school pupils, who are working in the nursery.

At Method II this category used for ancillary staff only. Working parents and other voluntary helpers coded separately:–

89 – Parents helping in the nursery
79 – Other helpers, e.g. secondary school children etc.

9 – PARENTS AND VISITORS: i.e. talking to parents, particularly when delivering or collecting children. Talking to visitors at school. Parents and visitors coded separately at Method II:
  9 – Parents
  99 – Visitors

* – STAFF GROUP: i.e. working with or talking to a mixed group of working adults.
Combination code 56 used to denote staff group at Method II.

Other combination codes used at Method II:
26 – mixed group children *and* staff
19 – mixed group children and parents

INITIATION CODES
These used at Method II only:
> – Self-Initiated change in activity
< – Other-Initiated change in activity

SCHEDULE FOR OBSERVING INDIVIDUAL STAFF

School Name _____ Staff Name _____ Date 14 - 7 - 76

School No: [1 2 3] Staff No: [3 0] Session No: [1] Sheet No: [0 3] Observer No: [2] Group No: [1]

1 2 3   4 5   6   7 8   9   10

Location No: [1] Resp. No: [2] No: Child. [4 0] No: Teachers [1] No: Assts. [2] No: Others [1]

11   12   13 14   15   16   17

	00	05	10	15	20	25	30	35	40	45	50	55
00	⌐Z 2											
01								⌐Z 2		<W 1	⌐Z 2	
02												
03									⌐S 1		<Z 1	
04												
05			⌐E 2									
06										⌐RT6		
07		<S 1		⌐S 1		<C 1		<W 1				
08			⌐H 0									
09												
10		⌐S 13										
11												
12				⌐Y 3								
13												
14												

ARD:3
Verbalization of individual staff in specified contexts

From the beginning of the study is was apparent that a detailed analysis of speech addressed to children was likely to provide invaluable information about differences between staff. Such speech can only be coded retrospectively. Accordingly was recorded by linking the radio-microphones to Philips Pocket-Memo Recorders. For each session, two continuous 15-minute samples of speech were recorded in parallel with ARD:2 observations, yielding one hour of recording for each of the 40 teachers and 40 assistants. The recordings were made during 'activity-time', which it was judged would provide most examples of speech in the three behavioural contexts selected for study: supervision, conversation and involvement with children's activities.

ARD:4

	School	Staff		Date			Session	

1 2 3 4 5   6 7 8 9 10 11 12

Aims, Role and Deployment of Staff in the Nursery

Observer's checklist of equipment and activities made available each session

X	BOOKS	☐	13
K	PLAYCORNERS	☐	14
	imaginative play e.g. home corner, Wendy House hospital, shop, theatre	☐	15
	family play e.g. dolls, cots, prams, doll's house	☐	16
	hand instruments (shakers, bells, drums etc).	☐	17
	piano	☐	18
	record player/tape recorder	☐	19
	dressing up	☐	20
N	SAND, NATURAL SUBSTANCES	☐	21
	dry sand	☐	22
	wet sand	☐	23
	soil, mud etc.	☐	24
R	WATER PLAY	☐	25
G	PLASTIC PLAY	☐	26
	clay	☐	27

	plasticine	☐	28
	dough	☐	29
	pastry	☐	30
WW	WOODWORK	☐	31
DQ	COLOURING AND DRAWING	☐	32
	pencils	☐	33
	crayons	☐	34
	felt pens	☐	35
	chalks	☐	36
PQ	PAINTING AND PRINTING	☐	37
	brush painting	☐	38
	finger/foot painting	☐	39
	printing	☐	40
	comb and paste	☐	41
CQ	COLLAGE, CUTTING AND STICKING	☐	42
JQ	JUNK MODELLING	☐	43
T	FLOOR TOYS	☐	44
	large blocks and bricks	☐	45
	floor layouts, farm, trains	☐	46
Z	PUZZLES AND TABLE TOYS	☐	47
	matching and sorting e.g. number, colour, size and shape sets; fuzzy felts; jigsaws	☐	48
	manipulative, e.g. peg-boards, lacing, sewing, threading.	☐	49

P	PRIMARY SCHOOL SKILLS	☐	50
	reading	☐	51
	writing	☐	52
	number	☐	53
B	CONSTRUCTION TOYS	☐	54
	construction sets (lego, meccano etc).	☐	55
	small bricks and blocks	☐	56
J	WHEELED TOYS AND APPARATUS	☐	57
	push and pull toys (trucks, trolleys etc).	☐	58
	pedal toys	☐	59
	adventure toys (climbing frames, swings, tyres, ropes, seesaw, boxes, rockers etc).	☐	60
I	INVESTIGATION	☐	61
	pets	☐	62
	plants	☐	63
	colour and interest table	☐	64
	weather chart/calendar	☐	65
Y	STORY AND RHYMES	☐	66
D	DRAMA	☐	67
U	MUSIC	☐	68
V	TELEVISION/VISITING SPEAKERS	☐	69
	watching T.V.	☐	70
	visiting speaker	☐	71
CF	COOKING	☐	72

OUTINGS ▢ 73

to other school
facilities e.g. Library,
gym etc. ▢ 74

out of school, e.g. to
station, shops, play
areas, walks etc. ▢ 75

Card No.

4	0

79   80

ARD:5

		School	Staff
1	2	3	4	5

Aims, Role and Deployment of Staff in the Nursery

QUESTIONNAIRE FOR TEACHERS

Please complete the following questions. All the information you provide will be treated in the strictest confidence. Thank you.

1. **Personal Details**

    Please enter in the box the number alongside the appropriate entry

    Sex
Female	1
Male	2

    6

    Age Group
Under 20	1
20–24	2
25–34	3
35–44	4
45–54	5
over 55	6

    7

    Marital Status
Single	1
Married	2

    8

    Do you have any children?
Yes	1
No	2

    9

2. **Details of Training**

Please indicate which of the following qualifications you possess. (Please tick one or more of the boxes as appropriate)

National Nursery Examination Board (NNEB) Certificate	☐	10
Teaching Certificate	☐	11
Bachelor of Education (B.Ed)	☐	12
University Degree	☐	13
Post-graduate Certificate in Education	☐	14
Advanced Diploma in Education	☐	15
Higher Degree (e.g. M.A., Ph.D.)	☐	16
Others — please specify:	☐	17
	☐	18

When did you take the major part of your professional training? (Please enter in the box the number alongside the appropriate reply)

Before 1940   1

1940–44   2

1945–49   3

1950–54   4

1955–59   5   ☐   19

1960–64   6

1965–69   7

Since 1970   8

What was the duration of your teacher training?

1 year	1
2 years	2
3 years	3	☐	20
4 years	4

Which of the following courses were included as a major part of your teacher training?

Nursery	☐	21
Infant	☐	22
Junior	☐	23
Secondary	☐	24

If your initial training did not include a nursery component, have you attended a conversion course to prepare you for nursery work?

| Yes | 1 |
| No | 2 | ☐ | 25 |

If yes, please give brief details:

organising body .... | 26

approx. date .... | 27

duration .... | 28

3. **Teaching Experience**

How many years have you been teaching?

Under 1 year 1

1– 5 years 2

6–10 years 3　　　　　⬜　　29

11–20 years 4

Over 20 years 5

How many years have you been teaching children of nursery age?

Under 1 year 1

1– 5 years 2

6–10 years 3　　　　　⬜　　30

11–20 years 4

Over 20 years 5

Which of the following age groups have you also taught?
(Please tick one or more of the boxes as appropriate)

No other age groups　　　⬜　31

Infant age children　　　⬜　32

Junior age children　　　⬜　33

Secondary age children　　⬜　34

4. **Present Appointment**

Please enter in the box the number
alongside the appropriate reply.

*How many years continuous teaching have
you completed in this school?*

Under 1 year   1
 1– 5 years   2
 6–10 years   3
11–20 years   4   35
Over 20 years   5

Are you employed full-time?

Yes   1

No   2   36

If no, please indicate the number of
half-day sessions you are employed
per week   37

*What is your present position of
responsibility?*

Nursery School Headteacher   1

Nursery School Deputy Head   2

Teacher in Charge of Nursery
Unit attached to Primary
School   3

Teacher   4

Probationary Teacher   5   38

*Are you responsible for a class or group
of children?*

Yes   1

No   2   39

Present Appointment – *continued*

How many of your colleagues are you responsible for at the present time?

Teachers	(Please indicate number)	☐	40
Nursery Assistants	"	"	"	☐	41
Teaching students	"	"	"	☐	42
NNEB students	"	"	"	☐	43
Ancillary Staff	"	"	"	☐	44
None			☐	45

Have you attended any course of in-service training in the past 3 years?

Yes   1

No   2   ☐   46

If yes please give brief details

Organising body   47

Date   48

Duration   49

Topic   50

Are you a member of any organisation
concerned with nursery education (e.g.
British Association for Early Childhood Education?)

Yes   1
No   2   [   ]   51

If yes, please give brief details

....

....

....

....   52

Card No.
[5 | 0]
79   80

ARD:6

School   Staff

1	2	3	4	5

Aims, Role, and Deployment of Staff in the Nursery

QUESTIONNAIRE FOR NURSERY ASSISTANTS

Please complete the following questions. All the information you provide will be treated in the strictest confidence. Thank you.

1.   **Personal Details**

Please enter in the box the number alongside the appropriate entry

Sex

Female	1		
Male	2	☐	6

Age Group

Under 20	1		
20 – 24	2		
25 – 34	3		
35 – 44	4		
45 – 54	5		
over 55	6	☐	7

Marital Status

Single	1		
Married	2	☐	8

Do you have any children?

Yes   1

No   2   ☐   9

2.   **Details of Training**
     Please indicate which of the following qualifi-
     cations you possess (Please tick one or more of
     the boxes as appropriate)

National Nursery Examination   ☐   10
Board NNEB (Certificate)

State Registered Nurse (SRN)   ☐   11

Child Care Reserve (CCR)   ☐   12

No qualification   ☐   13

Others – please specify: ☐   14

When did you take the major part of your
professional training? (Please enter in the box
the number alongside the appropriate reply)

Before 1940   1

1940 – 44   2

1945 – 49   3

1950 – 54   4

1955 – 59   5   ☐   15

1960 – 64   6

1965 – 69   7

Since 1970   8

What was the duration of your nursery training?

1 year	1
2 years	2
3 years	3
4 years	4

16

For which types of work were you primarily trained? (Please tick one or more of the boxes as appropriate).

Hospital	17
Day Nursery	18
Residential Nursery	19
Nursery School/Class	20
Infant School	21

3.   **Work with Young Children**

How many years have you been working with young children?

Under 1 year	1		
1 – 4 years	2		
5 – 10 years	3	☐	22
11 – 20 years	4		
over 20 years	5		

How many years have you been working in nursery schools/classes?

Under 1 year	1		
1 – 4 years	2		
5 – 10 years	3		
11 – 20 years	4	☐	23
over 20 years	5		

In which of the following situations have you also worked? (Please tick one or more of the boxes as appropriate).

Hospital	☐	24
Day Nursery	☐	25
Residential Nursery	☐	26
Infant School	☐	27
Other	☐	28

4.　**Present Appointment**
Please enter in the box the number alongside
the appropriate reply.

*How many years continuous teaching have
you completed in this school?*

Under 1 year	1		
1 – 5 years	2		
6 – 10 years	3		
11 – 20 years	4		
over 20 years	5	☐	29

Are you employed full-time?

| Yes | 1 | ☐ | |
| No | 2 | ☐ | 30 |

If no, please indicate the number
of half-day sessions you are
employed per week.　　☐　31

*Are you responsible for a class or group of
children?*

| Yes | 1 | ☐ | |
| No | 2 | ☐ | 32 |

*How many of your colleagues are you respon-
sible for at the present time?*

Teachers(Please indicate number.)	☐	33
Nursery Assistants　　" 　　"	☐	34
Teaching Students　　"　　"	☐	35
NNEB Students　　"　　"	☐	36
Ancillary Staff　　"　　"	☐	37
None	☐	38

Have you attended any course of in-service training in the past 3 years?

Yes	1		
No	2	[ ]	39

If yes, please give brief details

Organising body		40
Date		41
Duration		42
Topic		43

Are you a member of any organization concerned with nursery education (e.g. British Association for Early Childhood Education)?

Yes	1		
No	2	[ ]	44

If yes, please give brief details

....
....
....
....
....   45

Card No.

6	0
79	80

ARD:7
The Responsibilities of Staff in the Nursery

School Staff

1 2 3 4 5

We are interested in the divisions of responsibility between the members of staff in your nursery. Examples of different types of nursery work are listed on the following pages. Please would you indicate the degree of responsibility you personally have for each example.

For each example, please circle the number in the appropriate column.

Example:

	Not normally engaged in by nursery staff	Little or no resp.	Some resp.	Major or total resp.	NFER USE Col No.
Arranging the Christmas party	1	2	③	4	
Liaising with College tutors	1	②	3	4	
Washing paintwork	①	2	3	4	

SUPERVISION, CARE AND WELFARE OF CHILDREN	Not normally engaged in by nursery staff	Little or no resp.	Some resp.	Major or total resp.	NFER USE Col No.
Supervising group *towards* various activities of day, story, lunch, garden	1	2	3	4	6
Supervising individuals or small groups around unit, suggesting activities to children	1	2	3	4	7
Arbitrating in disputes and disciplining where necessary	1	2	3	4	8
Observing and assessing children at play	1	2	3	4	9
Comforting distressed children	1	2	3	4	10
Giving first aid	1	2	3	4	11
Accompanying sick children home/hospital etc.	1	2	3	4	12
Organizing and assisting children in toileting and washing. Attending to wet or soiled children	1	2	3	4	13
Washing or bathing where required	1	2	3	4	14
Assisting children to dress; do up buttons; tie laces etc.	1	2	3	4	15

HOUSEWORK	Not normally engaged in by nursery staff	Little or no resp.	Some resp.	Major or total resp.	NFER USE Col No.
Arranging furniture (tables, chairs etc.)	1	2	3	4	16
Sweeping, mopping, general cleaning – table tops etc.	1	2	3	4	17
Cleaning toilets, wiping basins etc.	1	2	3	4	18
Washing equipment, paint pots, brushes and general washing up	1	2	3	4	19
Caring for pets and plants	1	2	3	4	20
Washing, ironing and repairing children's personal/dressing up clothes etc.	1	2	3	4	21
Preparing food for children (milk, lunch-time etc.) and setting tables	1	2	3	4	22
Preparing tea/coffee for staff	1	2	3	4	23
Maintaining and repairing of nursery equipment	1	2	3	4	24
General Caretaking (locking up etc.)	1	2	3	4	25

ADMINISTRATION	Not normally engaged in by nursery staff	Little or no resp.	Some resp.	Major or total resp.	NFER USE Col No.
Marking Registers	1	2	3	4	26
Checking numbers and ordering lunches	1	2	3	4	27
Collecting apple/biscuit money	1	2	3	4	28
Arranging admissions	1	2	3	4	29
Completing LEA/DES/ Medical records and returns	1	2	3	4	30
General correspondence	1	2	3	4	31
Purchasing Equipment	1	2	3	4	32
Ordering Supplies	1	2	3	4	33
Arranging special events (e.g. outings, parties)	1	2	3	4	34
Running the School Library	1	2	3	4	35

PLANNING AND ORGANIZATION OF CHILDREN'S ACTIVITIES	*Not normally engaged in by nursery staff*	*Little or no resp.*	*Some resp.*	*Major or total resp.*	*NFER USE Col No.*
Planning themes for the week or month	1	2	3	4	36
Organizing daily routine or timetable of play activities, outside play; story-time; milk time; music, local outings	1	2	3	4	37
Establishing rota of staff responsibility for areas of supervision and specific activities within timetable	1	2	3	4	38
Selecting the variety of activities for each session	1	2	3	4	39
Preparing and planning specific activities (e.g. story, craft work, cooking).	1	2	3	4	40
Choosing equipment for purchase or acquisition	1	2	3	4	41
Arranging displays and interest tables	1	2	3	4	42
Setting out and preparing equipment, e.g. table games; toys, paint, paper, craft materials, apparatus, garden toys	1	2	3	4	43
Replenishing materials, e.g. paper for easels, paint, glue.	1	2	3	4	44
Dealing with finished work; setting on one side; drying paintings etc.	1	2	3	4	45

SUPERVISION OF & INVOLVEMENT IN CHILDREN'S ACTIVITIES	*Not normally engaged in by nursery staff*	*Little or no resp.*	*Some resp.*	*Major or total resp.*	*NFER USE Col No.*
Participation in children's play and conversation	1	2	3	4	46
Guiding and assisting individuals or small groups in activities	1	2	3	4	47
Introducing and developing a specific activity with an individual or group of children	1	2	3	4	48
Developing pre-reading, writing and number skills	1	2	3	4	49
Taking responsibility for group in music or drama	1	2	3	4	50
Taking responsibility for telling story to group of children	1	2	3	4	51
Taking responsiblity for group outings	1	2	3	4	52
Supervising children in garden	1	2	3	4	53
Supervising children for lunch	1	2	3	4	54
Supervising children during rest-time	1	2	3	4	55

CONTACT WITH PARENTS, VISITORS, STUDENTS & OTHER STAFF	Not normally engaged in by nursery staff	Little or no resp.	Some resp.	Major or total resp.	NFER USE Col No.
Discussing with parents their children's progress and any problems.	1	2	3	4	56
Visiting homes of children	1	2	3	4	57
Greeting parents at beginning/end of sessions	1	2	3	4	58
Participating in nursery staff meetings	1	2	3	4	59
Supervising ancillary members of staff (Secretarial/Catering/Caretaking etc).	1	2	3	4	60
Supervising student-teachers and discussing their work with them	1	2	3	4	61
Supervising and assisting parents working in the nursery	1	2	3	4	62
Liaising with visitors to the school (e.g. LEA Advisers, College Tutors).	1	2	3	4	63
Supervising NNEB students and discussing their work with them	1	2	3	4	64
Supervising and assisting secondary school pupils and other helpers in the nursery	1	2	3	4	65

Card No.

7	0
79	80

THE RESPONSIBILITIES OF STAFF IN THE NURSERY

School   Staff

1	2	3	4	5

We are interested in the division of responsibility between the members of staff in your nursery. Examples of different types of nursery work are listed on the following pages.

Please would you indicate which member, or members of staff are *mainly* responsible for each example by putting a tick in their column. If several members of staff are equally responsible tick *all* the relevant columns.

Examples

	Not normally engaged in by nursery staff	Head of school or nursery unit	Nursery teachers	Nursery assistants	Student teachers	Student NNEBs	Ancillary staff	Parents and helpers	NFER USE Col. no.
Arranging the Christmas Party			✓	✓					
Liaising with College Tutors		✓							
Washing paintwork							✓		

SUPERVISION, CARE AND WELFARE OF CHILDREN	Not normally engaged in by nursery staff	Head of school or nursery unit	Nursery teachers	Nursery assistants	Student teachers	Student NNEBs	Ancillary staff	Parents and helpers	NFER USE Col. no.
Supervising group towards various activities of day, story, lunch, garden									6 / 7
Supervising individuals or small groups around unit, suggesting activities to children									8 / 9
Arbitrating in disputes and disciplining where necessary									10 / 11
Observing and assessing children at play									12 / 13
Comforting distressed children									14 / 15
Giving First Aid									16 / 17
Accompanying sick children home/hospital etc.									18 / 19
Organizing and assisting children in toileting and washing, attending to wet or soiled children									20 / 21
Washing or bathing where required									22 / 23
Assisting children to dress; do up buttons; tie laces etc.									24 / 25

HOUSEWORK	Not normally engaged in by nursery staff	Head of school or nursery unit	Nursery teachers	Nursery assistants	Student teachers	Student NNEBs	Ancillary staff	Parents and helpers	NFER USE Col. no.
Arranging furniture (tables, chairs, etc.)									26 / 27
Sweeping, mopping, general cleaning – table tops etc.									28
Cleaning toilets, wiping basins etc.									29
Washing equipment, paint pots, brushes and general washing up									30 / 31
Caring for pets and plants									32 / 33
Washing, ironing and repairing children's personal/dressing-up clothes etc.									34 / 35
Preparing food for children (milk, lunch-time etc.,) and setting tables									36 / 37
Preparing tea/coffee for staff									38 / 39
Maintaining and repairing of nursery equipment									40 / 41
General caretaking – (locking up etc.)									42 / 43 / 44 / 45

ADMINISTRATION	Not normally engaged in by nursery staff	Head of school or nursery unit	Nursery teachers	Nursery assistants	Student teachers	Student NNEBs	Ancillary staff	Parents and helpers	NFER USE Col. no.
Marking registers									46 / 47
Checking numbers and ordering lunches									48 / 49
Collecting apple/biscuit money									50 / 51
Arranging admissions									52 / 53
Completing LEA/DES/medical records and returns									54 / 55
General correspondence									56 / 57
Purchasing equipment									58 / 59
Ordering supplies									60 / 61
Arranging special events (e.g. outings, parties)									62 / 63
Running the school library									64 / 65

Card No.

8	0

79   80

School [ ] Staff [ ]

1 2 3 4 5

PLANNING & ORGANIZATION OF CHILDREN'S ACTIVITIES	Not normally engaged in by nursery staff	Head of school or nursery unit	Nursery teachers	Nursery assistants	Student teachers	Student NNEBs	Ancillary staff	Parents and helpers	NFER USE Col. no.
Planning themes for the week or month									6 / 7
Organizing daily routine or timetable of play activities, outside play, story time, milk time, music, local outings									8
									9
Establishing rota of staff responsibility for areas of supervision and specific activities within timetable									10 / 11
Selecting variety of activities for each session									12 / 13
Preparing and planning specific activities (e.g. story, craft work, cooking)									14 / 15
Choosing equipment for purchase or acquisition									16 / 17
Arranging displays and interest tables									18 / 19
Setting out and preparing equipment, e.g. table games, toys, paint, paper, craft materials, apparatus, garden toys									20
									21
Replenishing materials, e.g. paper for easels, paint, glue									22 / 23
Dealing with finished work; setting on one side, drying paintings etc.									24 / 25

SUPERVISION OF & INVOLVEMENT IN CHILDREN'S ACTIVITIES	Not normally engaged in by nursery staff	Head of school or nursery unit	Nursery teachers	Nursery assistants	Student teachers	Student NNEBs	Ancillary staff	Parents and helpers	NFER USE Col. no.
Participation in children's play and conversation									26
									27
Guiding and assisting individuals or small groups in activities									28
									29
Introducing and developing a specific activity with an individual or group of children									30
									31
Developing pre-reading, writing and number skills									32
									33
Taking responsibility for group in music or drama									34
									35
Taking responsibility for telling story to group of children									36
									37
Taking responsibility group outings									38
									39
Supervising children in garden									40
									41
Supervising children for lunch									42
									43
Suprvising children during rest-time									44
									45

CONTACT WITH PARENTS, VISITORS, STUDENTS & OTHER STAFF	Not normally engaged in by nursery staff	Head of school or nursery unit	Nursery teachers	Nursery assistants	Student teachers	Student NNEBs	Ancillary staff	Parents and helpers	NFER USE Col. no.
Discussing with parents their children's progress and any problems									46 / 47
Visiting homes of children									48 / 49
Greeting parents at beginning/end of sessions									50 / 51
Participating in nursery staff meetings									52 / 53
Supervising ancillary members of staff (secretarial/ catering/ caretaking etc.)									54 / 55
Supervising student-teachers and discussing their work with them									56 / 57
Supervising and assisting parents working in the nursery									58 / 59
Liaising with visitors to the school (e.g. LEA Advisers, College Tutors)									60 / 61
Supervising NNEB students and discussing their work with them									62 / 63
Supervising and assisting secondary school pupils and other helpers in the nursery									64 / 65

Card No.

8 | 1

79   80

ARD:9

School Staff

1 2 3 4 5

INITIAL INTERVIEW WITH HEAD TEACHER

As a background to our observation in the nursery, we would like to have some information about the children attending the nursery and the members of nursery staff, students and other helpers, as well as learning something about your nursery organization and daily routine.

Firstly, please may we have details of all the adults we may meet during our visit to the nursery.

1. **Staffing**
   a) *Permanent staff (including ancillaries)*

Staff no.	Name	Position in nursery	Qualifi- cation	No. sessions attending	Other responsibilities & relevant details

Staff no. prefixes:
1. Head of School (always 10)
2. Teacher in charge/Deputy Head
3. Teachers
4. Assistants
5. Ancillaries

b) *Students*

Staff No.	Name	Type of Training	Year	No. sessions attending	Other relevant details

Staff no. prefixes
    6.   Student Teachers
    7.   Student NNEB's

c) *Other helpers (Parents, Secondary pupils, Voluntary Workers)*

Staff no.	Name	Position in nursery (e.g. parent)	Number sessions attending	Other relevant details

Staff no. prefixes:
    8.   Parents and other helpers

2. Grouping

a) We would like to know how the children are grouped in the nursery.

Please give details of the groups:

Group no.	No. children full-time	No. children part-time	Permanent staff in order of resp. (I.D. nos)	Students allocated to group (I.D. nos)	Other helpers (I.D. nos)	Other details

b) We would also like to know how groups are located in relation to each other and whether for *most of the day* they function independently or in conjunction with each other.

Diagram:

Key:

	Independent	Interacting
Building	───────────	-----------
Room	∧∧∧∧∧∧∧∧	/ / / /
Group	ℓℓℓℓℓℓℓℓℓℓ	o O o O o O o

3. **Organization of staff**
    a) Do the permanent staff remain with the group of children
        for at least a year?

        Yes
        No

        If not what is the pattern of rotation (details)
        Termly
        Monthly
        Weekly
        Other
    b) Do the students remain with a group of children for at least
        a year?

        Yes
        No

        If not give details

    c) Do the other helpers stay with a group of children?

        Yes
        No

        If not give details

4. **Organization of Programme**
   We would like to know about your daily routine.
   a) Is there a 'timetable' for the session?
      Give details:

   b) Are there set times for specific activities:
      milk, outside play, ?

   c) Are there formal group times for story, music etc?

   d) Is there a rota of staff responsibilities for these activities?

Organization of Programme – *contd.*

    e)   What is the planning process for the nursery?
           For example, how is your daily routine decided?
           (Cover responsibility/procedure etc.)

    f)   How much 'forward planning' for the week/term do you
           find necessary and how is this done?
           (Cover responsibility/procedure etc.)

    g)   Do you have staff discussion times?
           (Cover when, in what form and which staff members
           attend)

    h)   (Nursery classes only)
           Are staff meetings in the infant school attended by nursery
           staff? Which members of staff attend?

5. **Nursery Roll**

   a) What is the maximum number of places available each session?

   Morning session

   Afternoon session

   b) What is the total number of full-time/part-time places?

   No. full-time

   No. part-time

   c) Please enter in the table below the approximate numbers of children at present on the attendance register in the age groups given.
   (If none, put NONE)

Age	Under 2 years	2 yrs. but under 3	3 yrs. but under 3½	3½ yrs. but under 4	4 yrs. but under 4½	4½ yrs. but under 5	5 yrs. but under 6
No:							

ARD:10

GUIDELINES FOR INDIVIDUAL STAFF INTERVIEW

Role

1. *Reasons for entering nursery work*
   a) When?   Initial choice straight from school or interest developed later (cover history).
   b) Why?   Reasons behind choice:
      Teachers – Nursery/school class not primary school
      NNEB's   Nursery school/class not day nursery, residential nursery or hospital.

2. *Training – attitude to adequacy in light of practical experience* (Details, views etc).

3. *Perception of own position in nursery*
   a) *In relation to other staff:*
      personal status and degree of responsibility,
      working situation – co-operation, opinion differences etc.
      delegation of authority,
      use of parents/students etc.
      effect of being part of infant school (teacher part of team; NNEB's minority group).
   b) *In relation to nursery organization and planning*
      planning procedures – traditional methods
                – decision of those in responsibility
                – staff discussion
                – amount of personal contribution and influence.
   c) *In relation to job satisfaction, personal commitments, future prospects*
      satisfied with present situation – fits in well with personal commitments;
      sees present situation as experience to further career elsewhere;
      future prospects, promotion (effect of being part of infant school)

4. *View of present system of staffing in nursery education*
> need for change?
> affect of local/national developments (or lack of them) on aspects of work, personal position, prospects etc.

Aims and Objectives

5. *What are you trying to give the children through nursery education?*
    a) opportunities
    b) advantages
    c) abilities (hope/expect children will be able to do by the time they leave).

6. *How is your nursery organized to achieve this?*
> Rationale behind: timetable?
>   „   „   development of themes – out of school preparation?
>   „   „   leaving daily programme flexible?
>   „   „   involving children in specific activities?
>   „   „   grouping children for specific activities?
> Meeting individual needs of children.
>
> *Views on aspects of staff behaviour in the nursery (related to observation categories)*
    i)   importance of areas of staff activity
    ii) those that demand adult attention.
    iii) those that require adult involvement.

7. *Influences and constraints on the success of your work in the nursery?*
> district/location of school
> building/general facilities
> staffing
> children (background, knowledge of language etc).
> *outside pressures/policies:* LEA, adviser, parents, etc.
> *within nursery pressures/policies* – those in responsibility.

8.   *Future of nursery education*
           – co-ordination of education and care provision for under-
               fives.
           – integration with infant school (continuous process)?

INDIVIDUAL STAFF INTERVIEW

School   Staff

1   2   3   4   5

Role

1.   *Reasons for entering nursery work*

2.   *Training – attitude to adequacy in light of practical experience*

3.   *Perception of own position in nursery*

     a)   *In relation to other staff*

     b)   *In relation to nursery organization and planning*

   c) *In relation to job satisfaction, personal commitments, future prospects*

4. *View of present system of staffing in nursery education*

Aims and Objectives

5. *What are you trying to give the children through nursery education?*

6. *How is your nursery organized to achieve this?*

7. *Influences and constraints on the success of your work in the nursery*

8. *Future of nursery education*

Addendum to Appendix (A)

Observation instrument characteristics: ARD:1 – ARD:2

The validity of the observation system must be judged in terms of what it purported to measure, since measures of predictive validity, whilst much to be preferred, demanded a process-product study. The validity of the system was thus a 'content' validity analogous to that quoted for certain psychological tests, for instance of attitudes, where the user must consider the explicit nature of the questions, individually and collectively, and decide whether or not they do measure what they purport to measure. For observation systems, 'content' validity demands that the significant, as distinguished from the non-significant phenomena be included, and that *all* the significant phenomena be there.

A small pilot study was undertaken to establish the reliability of the observation system. The measures in which there was interest were of *inter-observer agreement:* the degree to which there was accord over categorization; and *staff consistency*: the degree to which what was observed was typical of the member of staff in question.

The following reliability measures were obtained:
1. Inter-observer reliability using Method I,
2. Inter-observer reliability using Method II,
3. The effect of radio-microphones on staff language,
4. The effect of observer presence on staff behaviour, using Method II.

1. *Inter-observer reliability using Method I*

The three members of the team went into a nursery in pairs, each member working in turn which each of the other two. Each pair spent one half-day session in the same school. Four members of staff were observed sequentially every two minutes. Each observation sheet covered 20 minutes and contained 40 Activity entries and 40 Context entries. The observations of each pair were later compared in terms of:
1. ACTIVITY entries
2. CONTEXT entries
All three pairs reached greater agreement on CONTEXT than ACTIVITY.

Observer	No. of Entries	Context Agreement	Activity Agreement
A/B	240	219	212
		91%	88%
C/B	160	145	134
		91%	84%
C/A	240	217	215
		90%	90%

Table 1: Summary of Agreement at Method I

The majority of ACTIVITY disagreements were in two areas:

(i) distinguishing between adult talk and administration. This problem was overcome by agreeing that adult talk (T) should be recorded whenever staff engaged in talk for its own sake. Where the talk was an intrinsic part of an activity such as administration, the activity itself should be coded.

(ii) distinguishing between conversation and other categories such as supervision, welfare, and involvement. This was resolved by sharpening the definition of conversation as that which occurs *outside* the context of any on-going activity (conversation for its own sake). Where the conversation was an integral part of another activity, that activity code was recorded.

2. *Inter-observer reliability using Method II*

Members of the team went into nurseries in pairs, each member working in turn with each of the other two. Each pair spent two half-day sessions in the same school, observing one member of staff at each session, one being a teacher and the other being an assistant.

Between nine and 11 observation sheets, each covering 15 minutes, were completed by each pair. The observations were later compared in terms of:

a) COMMON ENTRIES, i.e. agreement between observers on what to record.

b) AGREEMENT within entries in terms of –
    1. initiation
    2. activity
    3. context

Inter-observer agreement on categorization; what to record, was between 80 per cent and 86 per cent.

Observers	Sheets	Total Entries	Common Entries	Common Entries as % of Total Entries
C/B	11	224	191	85%
B/A	9	269	232	86%
A/C	9	316	252	80%

Table 2: showing common entries as percentage of total entries

The main sources of discrepancy were brief interruptions and asides, which were recorded by one observer and omitted by the other. Most of the asides consisted of short conversations and supervisory remarks to individual children. These accounted for between 30 per cent and 50 per cent of all omissions. Most other asides were brief instances of adult talk, which accounted for between 11 per cent and 30 per cent of all omissions.

It was decided that to resolve this problem 'interruptions and asides' of less than five seconds duration should not be recorded. This decision reflected our general view that such interruptions and asides were of little or no importance.

Inter-observer agreement was highest for the categorization of initiation, and lowest on activity:

Observers	Common Entries	Agreements as % of Common Entries		
		Initiation	Activity	Context
C/B	191	171 90%	163 85%	169 88%
B/A	232	199 86%	181 78%	196 84%
A/C	252	234 93%	219 87%	226 90%

Table 3: showing percentage of agreement on common entries

The main difficulties with the categorization of CONTEXT were in distinguishing between 1 and 2 (individual child, small group) and between 2 and 3 (small group and large group). The first was resolved by agreeing that where the context was not clear, the observer should record the *main* focus of the adult's attention. The second was dealt with by clarifying our definitions of 'small or informal', and 'large or formal'.

Disagreements over ACTIVITY categorization were of two main kinds. As in Method I, there was a disagreement over what constituted conversation, and other categories such as supervision, welfare and involvement. This accounted for almost half of all disagreement, and was resolved in the same way as in Method I. The second area of disagreement was in categorizing the content of adult talk. The subdivisions of T were therefore expanded to be more consistent with existing codes for staff behaviour.

3. *The effect of radio-microphones on staff language*

In order to measure what, if any, the effect of the wearing of a radio-microphone had on staff language, one teacher and one nursery assistant were observed separately by two members of the team. Each was observed for one hour WITHOUT the radio-microphone, and instances and durations of speech were recorded on Method II observation sheets. The same members of staff were again observed on the following day for the same length of time WITH the radio-microphone. Observations took place during the second half of the morning session on both occasions, so that the range of activities engaged in by the staff were as similar as possible.

The observations were then compared in terms of:
1. Percentage of total time spent in speech.
2. Average number of instances of speech per minute.
3. Average duration of instances of speech.

Any time spent in taking formal groups, e.g. story telling, was not included in the analysis.

In both cases, the staff members spent more time in speech when wearing the radio-microphone. The teacher engaged in more instances of speech which tended to be of shorter duration. The nursery assistant, on the other hand, engaged in fewer instances of speech but these were of longer duration, and this trend was consistent throughout the time she was observed.

4. *The effect of observer presence on staff behaviour, using Method II*

Two nursery assistants were observed using Method II. Each

was observed for one hour on each of three consecutive days, one in the morning and one in the afternoon. It was our expectation that the observer effect (if any) would be greatest during the first day, and would diminish with increasing familiarity.

The behaviour of each assistant was compared for each of the three observation periods, in terms of:

1. Number of changes of activity
2. Average duration of each activity
3. Percentage of total time spent in each activity category.

Nursery Assistant	Day	Changes of Activity	Av. Duration of each Activity
1	1	159	23 seconds
	2	106	34 seconds
	3	104	35 seconds
2	1	115	31 seconds
	2	136	26 seconds
	3	112	32 seconds

Table 4: showing observer effect on changes and average durations of areas of staff activities

The behaviour of Nursery Assistant I was more consistent on days 2 and 3 in all respects (see Table 4). The pattern was similar both for changes and average durations of activity, and for percentage of total time spent in each activity.

Observer effect, however, cannot be separated from other influences, e.g. variations in timetable, staffing and responsibility.

The behaviour of Nursery Assistant 2 shows a similarity in changes and average durations of activity between days 1 and 3 (see Table 5), but very little similarity in patterns of time spent in each activity over the three days. Influences other than the presence of the observer are clearly having an effect, e.g. the arrival of new pupils with their parents on day 2 and an accident on day 3.

It therefore appeared to us that any effect the observer might have on staff behaviour was likely to be obscured by the stronger influences of day-to-day changes or disruptions in nursery routine.

Apart from the question of whether the observation system was well enough refined to permit reliable categorization of events by several different observers at different times and in different places, the reliability of the data collected is also critically affected by how consistent is the behaviour of those observed.

Underlying the whole strategy of observational studies of human behaviour is the *assumption* that a sample of behaviour observed at a representative time and in a representative place will characterize behaviour at all such times and in all such places. Thus simply to demonstrate acceptable inter-observer agreement and lack of observer effect, whilst necessary, is not sufficient. It is also necessary to demonstrate that the behaviour being recorded is consistent; that is representative.

To this end, one teacher and one nursery assistant were each observed on Method II for one hour on three consecutive Fridays. The teacher was observed during the first half of the morning sessions and the assistant during the first half of the afternoon sessions throughout the three week period.

Behaviour was then compared for each member of staff in terms of the percentage of total time spent in each activity category over the three observation periods.

The nursery assistant

The nursery assistant's behaviour showed consistency over the three weeks in the activities engaged in most frequently (involvement and welfare) and those seldom or never engaged in during these periods. The three sessions were similar in terms of her responsibility, timetable, location, and even the weather. Since there were few changes or disruptions, each observation period can be taken to represent her 'normal' routine. (Note: the effect of the observer cannot be separated in this study of staff consistency.)

The teacher

This teacher was responsible for the nursery in the absence of the head on all three occasions. There was no obvious pattern of consistency in her behaviour. Week 1 showed a fairly routine morning. The differences between Week 1 and 2 showed the effect of the rota system operating in this nursery. (Duties were alternated between the teacher and her assistant.) Week 3 showed another pattern, since the nursery routine has been disrupted by the presence of the optician.

Clearly consistency of staff behaviour is affected by changes and disruptions in day-to-day routine as well as the effects of rotas and organization of responsibilities, and this has to be borne in mind when considering the results of the study. However, since the data on individuals is aggregated within types of adult (e.g. *all* nursery teachers, *all* nursery assistants etc.) for most of the analyses, there will be a tendency for the effect of routine variability to 'randomize out'.

Appendix B

Table 1: Percentage responsibility of different types of working adults in classes, schools and units in relation to different areas of nursery work

Nursery classes (N = 26)

Area of work	T.-in-charge (N = 26)	Teachers (N = 0)	N. Assts. (N = 26)	Student Ts. (N = 2)	Student Ns. (N = 12)	P.Sch.St. (N = 26)	Parents etc. (N = 11)
Supervision	95%		82%	83%	58%	8%	12%
Welfare	70%		92%	67%	51%	9%	12%
Housework	55%		73%	40%	43%	24%	12%
Administration	57%		8%	10%	1%	45%	–
Planning	98%		43%	90%	27%	2%	–
Equipment	92%		78%	60%	50%	–	9%
Involvement	99%		71%	57%	50%	2%	25%
Adult talk	84%		32%	22%	6%	18%	–

Nursery schools (N = 9)

Area of work	Head (N = 9)	Teachers (N = 8)	N.Assts. (N = 9)	Student Ts. (N = 3)	Student Ns. (N = 7)	Own Ancil. (N = 9)	Parents etc. (N = 5)
Supervision	82%	89%	95%	79%	61%	–	6%
Welfare	84%	73%	86%	39%	64%	–	20%
Housework	48%	46%	81%	33%	61%	41%	28%
Administration	92%	21%	12%	–	–	22%	4%
Planning	82%	70%	38%	33%	29%	–	–
Equipment	73%	98%	91%	47%	40%	–	12%
Involvement	92%	89%	67%	57%	33%	–	6%
Adult talk	99%	50%	31%	4%	3%	1%	–

Nursery units (N = 5)

Area of work	T-in-charge	Teachers (N = 5)	N.Assts. (N = 5)	Student Ts. (N = 2)	Student Ns. (N = 3)	P.Sch.St. (N = 5)	Parents etc. (N = 4)
Supervision	97%	97%	87%	50%	61%	3%	17%
Welfare	83%	76%	86%	50%	61%	4%	4%
Housework	50%	46%	80%	25%	63%	24%	10%
Administration	63%	37%	2%	–	–	33%	–
Planning	100%	72%	24%	50%	13%	–	–
Equipment	96%	100%	80%	70%	67%	–	–
Involvement	100%	100%	70%	71%	48%	–	14%
Adult talk	89%	62%	36%	–	–	10%	–

The division of responsibility between working adults in relation to individual areas of nursery work

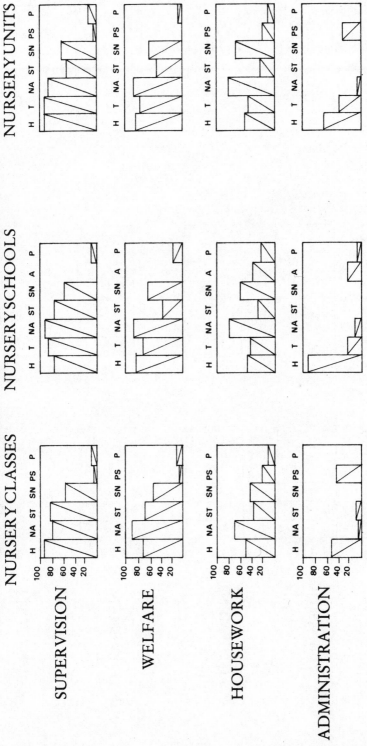

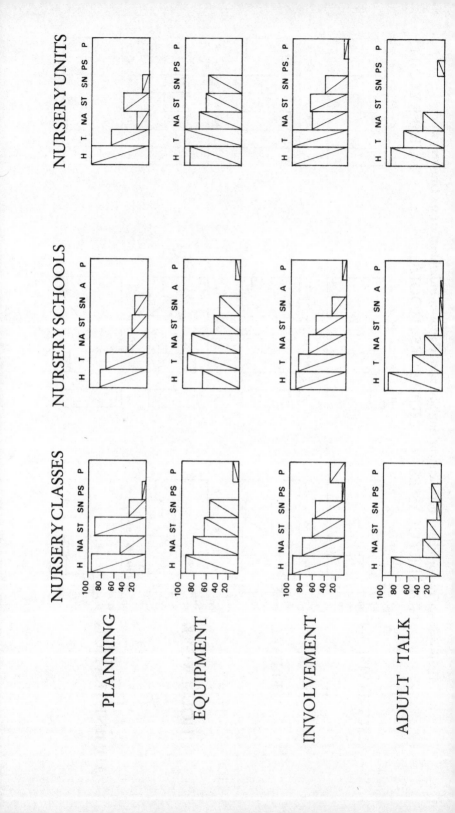

Appendix C

Table 1: Analysis of the time spent by teachers and nursery assistants in a two and a half-hour period, by activity, initiation and context

	Nursery Teachers %	Nursery Assistants %	All %
A			
Activity			
Involvement	45	38	41
Active supervision	20	17	18
Organizing equipment	8	11	10
Adult talk	9	8	10
Welfare	6	7	6
Conversation	7	6	6
Housework	2	10	6
Administration	2	1	2
Passive supervision	1	2	1
	100%	100%	100%
B			
Context			
Working with children	79	71	75
Working alone	10	19	15
Working with other adults	11	10	10
	100%	100%	100%
C			
Initiation			
Self	82	84	83
Other	18	16	17
	100%	100%	100%

Table 2: Average number of changes in activity made by teachers and nursery assistants in a two and a half-hour period analysed by new activity, initiation and context

	Average Number per Teacher	Average Number per Assistant	Average Number
A			
Activity			
Involvement	43	34	39
Active supervision	54	49	51
Organizing equipment	14	20	17
Adult talk	25	26	25
Welfare	13	15	14
Conversation	17	15	16
Housework	5	12	8
Administration	3	1	2
Passive supervision	3	2	3
	176	174	175
B			
Context			
Working with children	136	123	129
Working alone	26	27	27
Working with other adults	13	23	18
	176	174	175
C			
Initiation			
Self	124	125	124
Other	52	49	51
	176	174	175

Appendix D

DISCRIMINANT ANALYSIS[1]

Discriminant analysis begins with the desire to distinguish between two or more groups of cases. These 'groups' are defined by the particular research situation, in this instance nursery teachers and assistants.

To distinguish between the groups, a collection of *discriminating* variables that measure characteristics on which the groups are expected to differ are selected, in this instance the durations, frequencies and mean durations of staff involvement in nursery activities.

The mathematical objective of discriminant analysis is to weight and linearly combine the discriminating variables in such a way that the groups are forced to be as statistically distinct as possible. This is achieved by forming one or more linear combinations of the discriminating variables. These 'discriminant functions' are in the form of

$$D_i = d_{i1} Z_1 \times d_{12} Z_2 + \ldots d_{ip} Z_p$$

Where D_i is the score of the discriminant function i;
d's are the weighting coefficients;
Z's are the standardized values of the discriminating variables used in the analysis.

Once the discriminant functions have been derived they may be applied in two ways: *analysis* and *classification*. Regarding analysis, the success with which the discriminating variables actually discriminate when combined into the function(s) may be measured. Regarding classification, a set of classification functions can be derived which will permit the classification of new cases of unknown membership, as well as classifying the original set of cases to see how many were correctly classified by the variables used. In this instance the percentage of teachers, assistants, and overall staff correctly classified is presented, together with a Chi-squared test of significance of discrimination. For each discriminant analysis three tables are presented:

a) a summary table of the activity measures included;
b) the standardized discriminant function coefficients of the

---

[1]SPSS New York: McGraw Hill, 1975, pages 434-67.

activity measures included, on the basis of the absolute magnitude of which they may be placed in order of discriminating power;

c) the prediction results for each discriminant function.

Table 1: Activity durations

(A) Summary table

STEP NUMBER	VARIABLE ENTERED	VARIABLE REMOVED	F TO ENTER OR REMOVE	NUMBER INCLUDED	WILKS LAMBDA	SIG.	RAOS V	CHANGE IN RAOS V	SIG.
1	DV1		50.39881	1	.75816	.000	50.39881	50.39881	.000
2	DV3		11.02891	2	.70840	.000	65.03838	14.63957	.000
3	DV2		5.50589	3	.68425	.000	72.91033	7.87195	.005
4	DV4		.59718	4	.68162	.000	73.79998	.88965	.346
5	DV6		.61170	5	.67893	.000	74.72071	.92072	.337
6	DV7		.30253	6	.67759	.000	75.18087	.46016	.498

Activities not included:

Involvement in children's activities;
Welfare;
Passive supervision

1 Housework
2 Organization of equipment
3 Administration
4 Adult talk
5 Supervision
6 Conversation with children

(B) Standardization discriminant function coefficients

DV1	.84845
DV2	.33204
DV3	-.49591
DV4	-.14997
DV6	-.11070
DV7	.08143

(C) Prediction Results

ACTUAL GROUP NAME	CODE	N OF CASES	PREDICTED GROUP MEMBERSHIP GROUP 1	GROUP 2
GROUP 1 (Teachers)	-3	80	69. 86.2 PCT	11. 13.7 PCT
GROUP 2 (Assistants)	-2	80	26. 32.5 PCT	54. 67.5 PCT

76.9 PER CENT OF KNOWN CASES CORRECTLY CLASSIFIED

CHI-SQUARE = 46.225   SIGNIFICANCE = .000

Table 2: Activity frequencies

(A) *Summary table*

STEP NUMBER	VARIABLE ENTERED	VARIABLE REMOVED	F TO ENTER OR REMOVE	NUMBER INCLUDED	WILKS LAMBDA	SIG.	RAOS V	CHANGE IN RAOS V	SIG.
1	FV1		43.59725	1	.78374	.000	43.59725	43.59725	.000
2	FV3		21.70359	2	.68856	.000	71.46594	27.86869	.000
3	FV9		9.51313	3	.64898	.000	85.45914	13.99320	.000
4	FV2		6.80483	4	.62169	.000	96.14751	10.68837	.001
5	FV5		.61456	5	.61922	.000	97.16172	1.01421	.314
6	FV8		.19970	6	.61841	.000	97.49477	.33305	.564
7	FV7		.16658	7	.61773	.000	97.77477	.28000	.597
8	FV4		.15113	8	.61711	.000	98.00076	.25599	613

Activities not included:

Supervision

(B) *Standarization discriminant function coefficients*

FV1	.64334	Housework
FV2	.36806	Organization of equipment
FV3	-.64693	Administration
FV4	.05555	Adult talk
FV5	-.15359	Passive supervision
FV7	.06866	Conversation with children
FV8	-.05470	Welfare
FV9	-.36006	Involvement in children's activities

(C) *Prediction Results*

ACTUAL GROUP NAME	CODE	N OF CASES	PREDICTED GROUP MEMBERSHIP GROUP 1	GROUP 2
GROUP 1 (Teachers)	-3	80	68. 85.0 PCT	12. 15.0 PCT
GROUP 2 (Assistants)	-2	80	16. 20.0 PCT	64. 80.0 PCT

82.5 PER CENT OF KNOWN CASES CORRECTLY CLASSIFIED

CHI-SQUARE = 67.600   SIGNIFICANCE = .000

Table 3: Mean duration of activities (episodes)

(A) *Summary table*

STEP NUMBER	VARIABLE ENTERED	VARIABLE REMOVED	F TO ENTER OR REMOVE	NUMBER INCLUDED	WILKS LAMBDA	SIG.	RAOS V	CHANGE IN RAOS V	SIG.
1	MV1		12.67237	1	.92575	.000	12.67237	12.67237	.000
2	MV3		6.42917	2	.88933	.000	19.66142	6.98905	.000
3	MV8		4.23462	3	.86583	.000	24.4405	4.82262	.028
4	MV4		1.32177	4	.85851	.000	26.04018	1.55614	.212
5	MV7		1.07123	5	.85258	.000	27.32037	1.28019	.258
6	MV2		1.22411	6	.84581	.000	28.80307	1.48270	.223
7	MV9		.53250	7	.84286	.000	29.45749	.65442	.419
8	MV6		.11783	8	.84220	.001	29.60378	.14628	.702
9	MV5		.04044	9	.84197	.002	29.65435	.05058	.822

(All activities included)

(B) *Standarization discriminant function coefficients*

MV1	.58362	Housework
MV2	-.25175	Organization of equipment
MV3	-.41925	Administration
MV4	.21052	Adult talk
MV5	-.4247	Passive supervision
MV6	.06907	Supervision
MV7	.27052	Conversation with children
MV8	-.46328	Welfare
MV9	.15509	Involvement in children's activities

(C) *Prediction Results*

ACTUAL GROUP NAME	CODE	N OF CASES	PREDICTED GROUP MEMBERSHIP GROUP 1	GROUP 2
GROUP 1 (Teachers)	-3	80	57. 71.2 PCT	23. 28.8 PCT
GROUP 2 (Assistants)	-2	80	27. 33.7 PCT	53. 66.2 PCT

68.8 PER CENT OF KNOWN CASES CORRECTLY CLASSIFIED

CHI-SQUARE = 22.500   SIGNIFICANCE = .000

Episodes of activities

The following block graphs show the actual distributions of episodes of the nine summary activities as categorized and observed by Method 2 (ARD:2 Appendix A).

It must be noted that the scale of durations used is not one of equal intervals:

it is:

five seconds or less duration;

six to 10 seconds duration;

11 to 15 seconds duration;

16 to 30 seconds duration;

31 to 60 seconds duration;

one+ to 2 minutes duration;

two+ to five minutes duration;

five+ to 10 minutes duration;

10+ minutes duration.

The effect of this unequal interval scale is to impart a rough pseudo symmetry about the mode,[1] (which was generally less than one minute), because the relatively rarer episodes which lasted for longer than the modal duration were aggregated into wide-span intervals of one minute, three minutes, five minutes and more than ten minutes. Each block graph represents the aggregate data from two separate nursery sessions, each adjusted (standardized) to two and a half hours. Since there were 40 teachers and 40 assistants involved in the study, each block graph thus represents 160 standardized sessions; 400 hours of observation. The block graphs are presented in the order of their importance to the discriminant function, reported on page 182, starting with the summary activity which differentiated most strongly between teachers and assistants, housework, and finishing with the one which differentiated the least, passive supervision.

Taking housework as an example, in 200 hours of observation, just over 90 (the mode) episodes of housework, each lasting between 16 and 30 seconds, were observed being done by teachers, and three episodes lasting for more than 10 minutes. By contrast, for example, just over 200 episodes (the mode) of housework, each lasting between 31 and 60 seconds were observed being done by assistants in 200 hours of observation.

---

[1]Mode: the score which occurs most often: the most *typical* score.

Housework

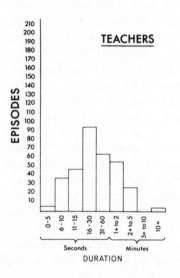

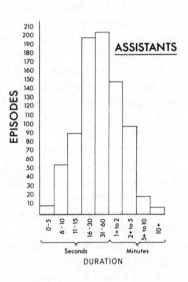

Welfare

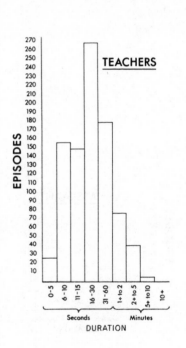

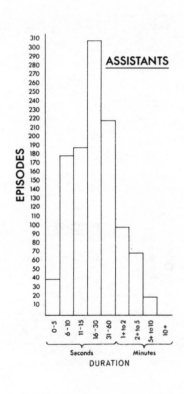

Administration

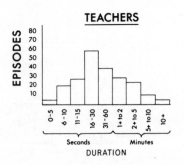

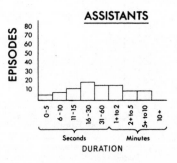

Conversation

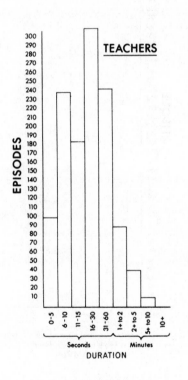

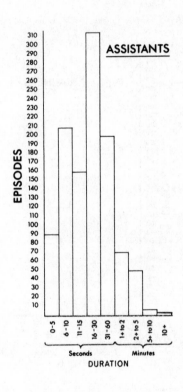

Equipment

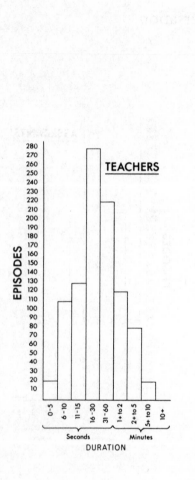

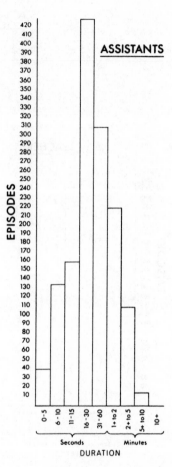

Adult Talk

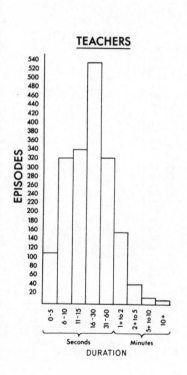

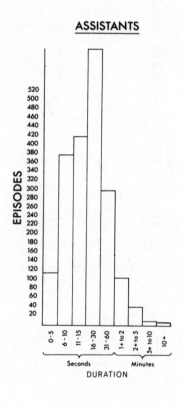

Involvement

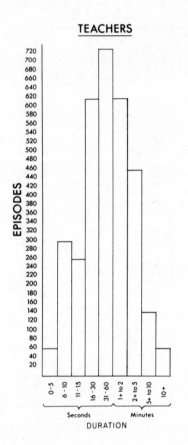

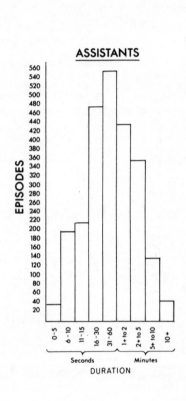

Supervision

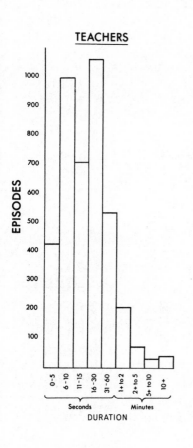

TEACHERS

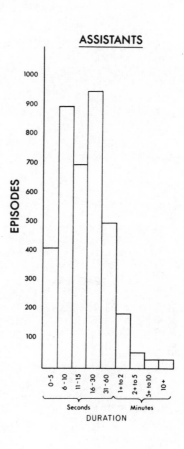

ASSISTANTS

Passive Supervision

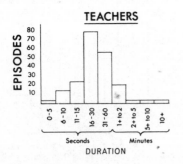

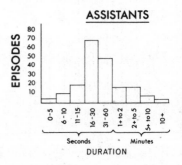

Table 4: The ranking of activities according to availability and adult involvement

Ranking of Activities According to Frequency of Availability	*Ranking of Activities According to Amount of Adult Involvement*
1. Books	1. Stories and rhymes
2. Playcorners	2. Puzzles/table toys
3. Investigation	3. Painting/printing
4. Puzzles/table toys	4. Collage/cutting
5. Painting/printing	5. Investigation
6. Sand	6. Music
7. Floor toys	7. Large apparatus/wheeled toys
8. Water	8. Cooking
9. Stories and rhymes	9. TV/visiting speaker
10. Large apparatus/wheeled toys	10. Floor toys
11. Construction toys	11. Colouring/drawing
12. Colouring/drawing	12. Books
13. Plastic play	13. Primary school skills
14. Collage/cutting	14. Playcorners
15. Music corner	15. Construction
16. Music	16. Plastic play
17. Junk modelling	17. Sand
18. Primary school skills	18. Junk modelling
19. TV/visiting speaker	19. Drama
20. Woodwork	20. Water
21. Drama	21. Woodwork
22. Cooking	22. Music corner.

Table 5: Table of involvement in individual activities

Significant differences between staff:

	Mean Ts	Mean Ns	Sig. Level
Books			
frequency	1.40	0.62	p<.05
duration	164.90	59.52	p<.05
mean duration	112.58	107.36	NS
Primary skills			
frequency	1.39	0.23	p<.05
duration	177.44	30.16	p<.05
mean duration	121.20	130.39	NS
Wheeled toys and apparatus			
frequency	2.60	1.55	p<.05
duration	179.59	125.47	NS
mean duration	65.93	78.25	NS
Investigation			
frequency	2.88	1.54	p<.05
duration	292.91	113.57	p<.01
mean duration	99.85	71.43	NS
Stories			
frequency	2.52	1.36	p<.001
duration	629.86	296.32	p<.01
mean duration	238.32	284.27	NS

Other involvement

Non-significant differences:

	Mean Ts	Mean Ns	Sig. Level
Playcorners			
frequency	2.26	2.38	NS
duration	114.86	101.74	NS
mean duration	48.21	42.68	NS
Music corner			
frequency	.04	-	NS
duration	2.12	-	NS
mean duration	42.00	-	NS

Sand	Mean Ts	Mean Ns	Sig. Level
frequency	.91	1.15	NS
duration	75.21	86.57	NS
mean duration	81.67	74.86	NS

Floor toys			
frequency	1.16	1.32	NS
duration	79.30	151.38	NS
mean duration	64.07	106.80	NS

Puzzles/table toys			
frequency	5.92	4.90	NS
duration	511.38	456.66	NS
mean duration	95.11	90.67	NS

Water			
frequency	.69	.67	NS
duration	42.72	40.16	NS
mean duration	64.26	58.11	NS

Plastic play			
frequency	1.61	1.17	NS
duration	79.13	103.91	NS
mean duration	49.04	84.16	NS

Woodwork			
frequency	.08	.22	NS
duration	6.01	17.35	NS
mean duration	77.00	73.61	NS

Colouring/drawing			
frequency	2.23	1.65	NS
duration	135.67	105.11	NS
mean duration	59.80	63.92	NS

Painting/printing			
frequency	5.71	4.53	NS
duration	406.36	259.10	NS
mean duration	70.73	55.68	NS

Collage/cutting	Mean Ts	Mean Ns	Sig. Level
frequency	4.17	3.81	NS
duration	276.70	313.32	NS
mean duration	67.15	82.72	NS

Junk modelling			
frequency	.94	1.30	NS
duration	84.11	76.27	NS
mean duration	87.95	59.63	NS

Construction			
frequency	1.74	1.44	NS
duration	91.70	104.12	NS
mean duration	53.21	72.89	NS

Drama			
frequency	.14	.20	NS
duration	55.25	50.23	NS
mean duration	355.42	250.33	NS

Music			
frequency	.61	.75	NS
duration	170.15	202.93	NS
mean duration	258.61	264.23	NS

TV/visiting speaker			
frequency	.28	.30	NS
duration	126.50	111.62	NS
mean duration	434.52	368.86	NS

Milk time			
frequency	1.57	.87	NS
duration	168.36	154.00	NS
mean duration	120.98	172.88	NS

Cooking			
frequency	.40	.96	NS
duration	103.53	187.59	NS
mean duration	254.83	185.14	NS

Party	Mean Ts	Mean Ns	Sig. Level
frequency	.04	.22	NS
duration	11.38	59.90	NS
mean duration	285.00	270.46	NS

Appendix E

Table 1: Summary of Speech Sequences Studied

1.   Nursery school teacher with small group.
       Collage/cutting: mosaic picture of the Queen.
       Adult utterances: 31
       Child utterances: 11

2.   Nursery school assistant with small group.
       Collage/cutting: crown of shells and pebbles.
       Adult utterances: 28
       Child utterances: 5

3.   Class teacher with small group.
       Collage/cutting: frieze of cut-out foot shapes.
       Adult utterances: 26
       Child utterances: 4

4.   Class assistant with small group.
       Collage/cutting: making paper hats.
       Adult utterances: 30
       Child utterances: 3

5.   Class teacher with small group.
       Table toys: matching game.
       Adult utterances: 30
       Child utterances: 7

6.   Class assistant with small group.
       Table toys: matching game.
       Adult utterances: 30
       Child utterances: 7

7.   Unit teacher with small group.
       Table toys: jigsaw puzzles.
       Adult utterances: 36
       Child utterances: 6

8.   Unit assistant with small group.
       Table toys: jigsaw puzzles.
       Adult utterances: 39
       Child utterances: 14

9.   Class teacher with small group.
        Construction: docks with Lego and Sticklebricks.
        Adult utterances: 30
        Child utterances: 19

10.   Class assistant with small group.
        Construction: docks with Sticklebricks.
        Adult utterances: 36
        Child utterances: 27

11.   Class teacher with individual child.
        Construction: house with small bricks.
        Adult utterances: 35
        Child utterances: 21

12.   Class assistant with small group.
        Construction: Lego cranes and fire engine.
        Adult utterances: 29
        Child utterances: 17

13.   Class teacher with small group.
        Plastic play: making pastry shapes.
        Adult utterances: 30
        Child utterances: 14

14.   Class assistant with small group.
        Plastic play: making pastry shapes.
        Adult utterances: 32
        Child utterances: 7

15.   Class teacher with small group.
        Water play: the water pump.
        Adult utterances: 30
        Child utterances: 1

16.   Class assistant with small group.
        Water play: the water pump.
        Adult utterances: 30
        Child utterances: 7

17.   Unit teacher with small group.
          Painting: sprinkling paint powder on pasted paper.
          Adult utterances: 22
          Child utterances: 8

18.   Unit teacher with small group.
          Painting: dribble-paint butterflies.
          Adult utterances: 20
          Child utterances: 11

19.   Class teacher with individual child.
          Playcorners: the Wendy House.
          Adult utterances: 26
          Child utterances: 6

20.   Class assistant with small group.
          Playcorners: shop.
          Adult utterances: 22
          Child utterances: 8

Table 2: Codes and categories of adult speech in children's activities

Responding to children

O	Makes general social remark
A1	Makes positive affective remark
A2	Makes negative affective remark
Y	Affirms child's statement
N	Negates child's statement
R	Corrects and makes simple extension of child utterance/ reinforces
E	Makes complex extension of child utterance
S	Provides summary of discussion/resumé

Directing behaviour

CS1	Makes simple positive control remark
CS2	Makes simple negative control remark
CC1	Makes positive control remark with explanation
CC2	Makes negative control remark with explanation
G	Sets goal
DS	Gives simple directions/demonstration
DC	Gives complex directions

Giving information

G1	Gives simple identification
GD	Gives simple description
GC	Gives simple comparison/relations
GR	Gives process report/description
GP	Gives projection outside situation
GL	Gives logical reasoning
GH	Gives hypothetical deduction

Requesting information

SQ	Requests quick decision (Yes/No)
S1	Requests simple identification
SD	Requests simple description
SC	Requests simple comparison/relation
SR	Requests report/description
SP	Requests projection outside situation
SL	Requests logical reasoning
SH	Requests hypothetical deduction

Examples
Responding to children

General social	Hello.
Affective	
(a) Positive	That is nice.
(b) Negative	That is horrid.
Affirms child's statement.	Yes
Negates child's statement.	No.
Corrects and makes simple extension to child statement/ reinforces	Yes, they do have big wheels.
Complex extension/elaboration	Yes, they do have big wheels and then they need big tyres to go on them.
Summary/resumé	We have been making a picture of the Queen and now it's finished we'll put it on the wall.

Directing behaviour

Simple control
(a) Positive   Please sit down.
(b) Negative   Don't stand up.

Control with explanation
(a) Positive   Please sit down, or you will fall.
(b) Negative   Don't stand up or you will fall.
Sets goal   Can you make the red pile the
                                same as the blue?
Gives simple directions/   Now, put another red one on.
demonstrates
Gives complex directions   Start by separating the bricks
                                into piles, then build up the red
                                pile until it is equal to the blue.

Giving information

Simple identification   It is a ball.
Simple description   It is a *red* ball.
                                 He kicked it *fast*.
Simple comparisons/ relations   There are three red balls – one is
                                 bigger than the others.
Process report/ description   The wheel fixes on with a nut.
Projections outside situation   Buses have big wheels too.
Logical reasoning   They have big wheels so they
                                 don't get stuck in the mud.
                                 Daddies are for earning money.
                                 We'll put the cakes in the oven
                                 then they will be cooked.
Hypothetical deduction   If they had little wheels they
                                 would get stuck.

Requesting information

Quick decision (Yes/No)   Can you see it?
Identification
(a) Personal   Who kicked the ball?
(b) Impersonal   What is he kicking?
(c) Action   What is he doing?
(d) Kind   Which ball is he kicking?

Description
(a) Type   What colour is the ball?
(b) State   How fast does it go?
(c) Time   When did he kick it?
(d) Space   Where did he kick it?

Comparisons/relation
(a) Similarities   What other red things can you
                                  see?
(b) Differences   Which is bigger?
                                  Which is biggest?

Process report description   How does this wheel fix on?

Projection beyond present   What other things have wheels?

Logical reasoning
(a) Causal   Why do tractors have big
                                  wheels?
(b) Effect   What are Daddies for?

Hypothetical deduction   What might happen if they had
                                  little wheels?

Sources

TIZARD, B., PHILPS, J. and PLEWIS, I. (1976). 'Staff behaviour in pre-school centres', *J. Child Psychology and Psychiatry*, **17**, 1, Jan, 21-33.

TIZARD, B., COOPERMAN, O., JOSEPH, A and TIZARD, J. (1972). 'Environmental effects on language development: a study of young children in long-stay residential nurseries', *Child Development*, **43**, 2, 337-58.

SCHOOLS COUNCIL (1975) A guide to the fostering of communication skills: a first draft (Joan Tough).

Appendix F

Note: In Tables 1 to 4 inclusive:

f is the average (mean) standardized frequency of involvement of the various listed adults in the various listed categories of activity, and sd is the standard deviation of these standardized frequencies.

Activity	(N)	Heads	(N)	Ts.in.Cb	(N)	Other Ts.	(N)	All Ts.	(N)	N.Assts	(N)	St.NNEB	(N)	Parents	(N)	All Staff
Total (N)	6		49		18		73		101		29		4		207	
Housework	6	f 2.97 sd 2.31	31	f 2.48 sd 3.29	11	f 4.91 sd 5.64	48	f 3.12 sd 4.02	98	f 11.07 sd 7.12	28	f 14.70 sd 14.56	2	f 10.25 sd 12.18	176	f 8.71 sd 8.95
Equipment	5	f 5.01 sd 3.57	48	f 6.22 sd 4.57	18	f 8.37 sd 4.75	71	f 6.65 sd 4.61	98	f 10.47 sd 6.17	28	f 10.41 sd 6.79	3	f 10.67 sd 7.82	200	f 9.07 sd 6.05
Administration	4	f 7.79 sd 11.66	37	f 1.91 sd 1.98	7	f 1.24 sd 2.47	48	f 2.23 sd 4.05	27	f .56 sd 1.25	0	f – sd –	0	f – sd –	75	f 1.06 sd 2.69
Adult talk	6	f 10.67 sd 7.30	47	f 5.70 sd 3.80	18	f 6.28 sd 4.05	71	f 6.25 sd 4.36	86	f 4.26 sd 3.66	20	f 2.30 sd 3.56	2	f 2.50 sd 3.32	179	f 4.63 sd 4.11
Supervision	6	f 8.17 sd 5.21	49	f 14.53 sd 6.62	18	f 9.61 sd 6.54	73	f 12.79 sd 6.90	99	f 8.48 sd 5.50	28	f 6.86 sd 6.27	3	f 6.33 sd 6.27	203	f 9.68 sd 6.34
Conversation	5	f 3.01 sd 1.72	38	f 3.85 sd 4.07	15	f 2.78 sd 2.78	58	f 3.52 sd 3.65	68	f 2.58 sd 3.49	18	f 2.21 sd 3.05	3	f 1.58 sd 1.71	147	f 2.83 sd 3.49
Welfare	4	f 3.33 sd 3.27	43	f 4.72 sd 4.93	14	f 4.30 sd 3.61	61	f 4.50 sd 4.49	89	f 6.71 sd 5.58	24	f 4.18 sd 3.52	3	f 2.67 sd 2.94	177	f 5.47 sd 5.05
Supportive	2	f .50 sd .84	9	f .80 sd 2.09	3	f .95 sd 2.66	14	f .81 sd 2.15	52	f 2.75 sd 4.09	19	f 6.67 sd 7.79	1	f .75 sd 1.50	86	f 2.56 sd 4.63
Responsibility	6	f 31.33 sd 13.24	49	f 26.59 sd 9.69	18	f 30.82 sd 12.77	73	f 28.02 sd 10.84	87	f 17.37 sd 12.15	27	f 18.36 sd 12.08	3	f 16.76 sd 18.39	191	f 21.22 sd 12.73
Garden	1	f .19 sd .47	27	f 5.51 sd 7.11	10	f 5.34 sd 7.72	38	f 5.03 sd 7.06	55	f 7.14 sd 11.50	14	f 5.53 sd 7.28	1	f 2.50 sd 5.00	108	f 6.05 sd 9.50

Table 1: ARD:1 – Individual activities

Table 2: ARD:1 – Grouped activities

	(N)	Heads	(N)	Ts.in.Ch	(N)	Other Ts.	(N)	All Ts.	(N)	N.Assts	(N)	St.NNEB	(N)	Parents	(N)	All Staff
Activities associated with children																
1. *Involvement* (Resp. & Supp.)	6	f 31.83 sd 12.73	49	f 27.39 sd 9.88	18	f 31.77 sd 12.33	73	f 28.83 sd 10.80	92	f 20.12 sd 12.23	28	f 25.03 sd 14.26	3	f 17.50 sd 18.19	197	f 23.78 sd 12.73
2. *Other contacts* (Welfare Super. Soc. Con.)	6	f 14.51 sd 4.85	49	f 23.10 sd 7.09	18	f 16.68 sd 8.43	73	f 20.81 sd 7.94	99	f 17.77 sd 8.50	28	f 13.24 sd 7.27	3	f 10.58 sd 7.37	203	f 17.98 sd 8.57
Activities associated with administration and organization																
(Housework, Org. Equip. Admin.)	6	f 15.77 sd 11.87	49	f 10.51 sd 5.81	18	f 14.51 sd 8.39	73	f 12.00 sd 7.28	99	f 22.09 sd 8.43	28	f 25.11 sd 15.97	3	f 20.92 sd 19.07	203	f 18.84 sd 11.02

Table 3: ARD:1 – Individual contexts

	(N)	Heads	(N)	Ts.in.Ch	(N)	Other Ts.	(N)	All Ts.	(N)	N.Assts	(N)	St.NNEB	(N)	Parents	(N)	All Staff
Self	6	f 19.72 sd 15.73	49	f 14.77 sd 8.55	18	f 14.98 sd 6.34	73	f 15.23 sd 8.79	101	f 26.00 sd 13.10	29	f 31.05 sd 16.76	4	f 43.08 sd 26.44	208	f 23.45 sd 14.47
Individual	6	f 15.82 sd 6.49	46	f 11.24 sd 7.90	18	f 9.54 sd 5.22	70	f 11.20 sd 7.31	95	f 10.18 sd 6.61	28	f 8.86 sd 5.13	3	f 5.83 sd 5.59	196	f 10.22 sd 6.72
Small group	6	f 19.68 sd 9.56	49	f 24.75 sd 12.05	18	f 29.62 sd 13.11	73	f 25.53 sd 12.30	97	f 24.11 sd 13.04	28	f 22.84 sd 14.10	3	f 19.08 sd 14.42	201	f 24.22 sd 12.99
Large group	5	f 13.95 sd 11.82	45	f 22.84 sd 12.52	17	f 17.24 sd 10.44	67	f 20.73 sd 12.24	91	f 13.47 sd 12.94	22	f 13.02 sd 10.96	2	f 8.00 sd 9.27	183	f 15.85 sd 12.80
Head	0	f – sd –	4	f .10 sd .37	11	f 1.38 sd 1.44	15	f .41 sd .94	40	f 1.12 sd 1.74	6	f .84 sd 2.10	1	f .25 sd .50	62	f .81 sd 1.58
Teacher	0	f – sd –	10	f .30 sd .66	3	f .25 sd .59	13	f .27 sd .62	37	f 1.09 sd 2.31	10	f .71 sd 1.08	3	f 1.33 sd .94	63	f .75 sd 1.74
Assistant	3	f 1.94 sd 3.11	40	f 1.99 sd 1.62	13	f 3.91 sd 5.10	56	f 2.46 sd 3.04	34	f .99 sd 1.95	15	f 2.28 sd 3.66	2	f 1.25 sd 1.50	107	f 1.69 sd 2.72
Students	0	f – sd –	7	f .43 sd 1.22	5	f .61 sd 1.14	59	f .44 sd 1.15	19	f .79 sd 2.37	2	f .11 sd .42	–	f – sd –	33	f .55 sd 1.81
Parents and visitors	6	f 8.29 sd 8.19	39	f 3.13 sd 3.25	11	f 2.12 sd 2.45	56	f 3.31 sd 3.94	52	f 1.63 sd 2.71	4	f .18 sd .48	1	f .25 sd .50	113	f 1.98 sd 3.19
Staff group	1	f .17 sd .41	3	f .10 sd .46	4	f .24 sd .46	8	f .14 sd .46	–	f .22 sd –	1	f .04 sd .21	–	f – sd –	19	f .16 sd .60

Table 4: ARD:1 – Grouped contexts

	(N)	Heads	(N)	Ts.in.Cb	(N)	Other Ts.	(N)	All Ts.	(N)	N.Assts	(N)	St.NNEB	(N)	Parents	(N)	All Staff
Contact with children	6	f 49.44 sd 17.59	49	f 58.83 sd 9.37	18	f 56.40 sd 10.21	73	f 57.46 sd 10.56	99	f 47.77 sd 12.67	28	f 44.72 sd 15.97	3	f 32.92 sd 24.17	204	f 50.29 sd 14.04
Contact with adults	6	f 10.84 sd 7.35	48	f 6.40 sd 3.84	18	f 8.62 sd 5.68	72	f 7.32 sd 4.82	90	f 6.23 sd 5.45	25	f 4.22 sd 4.76	3	f 4.00 sd 3.27	190	f 6.26 sd 5.19

Table 5: Significant differences between teachers and nursery assistants: ARD:1

Individual Activities	N	Teachers Av.St.Fr.	SD/St.Fr.	N	Assistants Av.St.Fr.	SD/St.Fr.	Sig. Level
Administration	48	2.23	4.05	27	.56	1.25	p<. 05
Adult talk	71	6.25	4.36	86	4.26	3.66	p<. 01
Responsibility	73	28.02	10.84	87	17.37	12.15	p<.001
Supervision	73	12.79	6.90	99	8.48	5.50	p<.001
Housework	48	3.12	4.02	98	11.07	7.12	p<.001
Equipment	71	6.65	4.61	98	10.47	6.17	p<.001
Welfare	61	4.50	4.49	89	6.71	5.58	p<. 05
Grouped Activities Activities associated with child: Responsibility	73	28.83	10.80	92	20.12	12.23	p<.001
Other contacts: (Sup/Soc.Con/ Welf.)	73	20.81	7.94	99	17.77	8.50	p<. 05
Act. assoc. with organ. (House/Equip/ Admin.)	73	12.00	7.28	99	22.09	8.43	p<.001
Individual Contexts Large gp. children	67	20.73	12.24	91	13.47	12.94	p<.001
Parents/vis.	56	3.31	3.94	52	1.63	2.71	p<. 01
Self	73	15.23	8.79	101	26.00	13.10	p<.001
Grouped Contexts Contacts with children	73	57.46	10.56	99	47.77	12.67	p<.001

Av. St. Fr. = Average (Mean) Standardized Frequency
SD/St. Fr. = Standard Deviation Standardized Frequency

Key to the Activity Codes featured in Tables 6, 7, 8.

R = Responsible for children's activities
  (R1– in the context of an individual child
   R2– in the context of a small group
   R3– in the context of a large group
U = Supportive in a group activity
H = Housework
E = Organization of equipment
G = Garden activities
C = Social conversation
W = Welfare
S = Supervision
  (S1– supervision of an individual child
   S2–   „   of a small group
   S3–   „   of a large group

Table 6: ARD:1 – Most frequently occurring patterns of deployment across teams of different size, (4, 3, 2 and 1 member).

4 member team				Stand. Freq.	Percentage Freq.	Cumul. Freq.
R3	U	H	H	17 }	2.507	2.507
R2	R2	C	E	17 }		
G	G	H	H	16 }	2.359	4.866
R2	R2	W	E	16 }		
R2	R2	R2	R2	12	0.884	5.750
R3	U	E	H	10 }		
R2	R2	R2	H	10 }	2.212	7.962
R3	R3	H	H	10 }		
R2	R2	R2	C	8 }	1.179	9.141
G	R2	R2	E	8 }		
3 member team						
R2	R2	R2		51	3.761	3.761
R3	U	U		41	3.023	6.784
R2	R2	H		31	2.286	9.070
G	H	H		24	1.769	10.839
G	G	E		23 }		
R3	H	H		23 }	5.088	15.927
R2	R2	E		23 }		
R3	E	H		20	1.474	17.401
R2	R2	R1		19	1.401	18.802
R2	R2	W		18	1.327	20.129
2 member team						
R3	H			93	6.858	6.858
R2	R2			71	5.235	12.093
R3	U			67	4.940	17.034
R3	E			63	4.646	21.680
R2	E			40 }		
R2	R1			40 }	8.849	30.529
R2	S2			40 }		
R2	C			34	2.507	33.036
G	H			31 }	4.472	37.608
R2	W			31 }		
1 member of staff working alone						
R3				301	22.197	22.197
E				184	13.569	35.766
R2				167	12.315	48.081
S3				154	11.356	59.437
S2				111	8.185	67.622
C				86	6.342	73.964
W				81	5.973	79.937
G				64	4.719	84.656
S1				60	4.424	89.080
H				51	3.761	92.841

To overcome differences in the number of observed instances of teams of different size, frequencies have been standardized on the basis that all teams occurred with equal frequency and had the same length of session. Comparison was limited to the top ten recurring patterns as, even within this number, the standardized frequencies of four-member teams fell within single figures, and talk about 'patterns' in relation to such small numbers would be meaningless. The cumulative frequencies indicate what percentage of the total behaviour of each team 10 patterns represent.

Table 7: Contributory activities   ARD:1

The activities that contribute to the ten most frequently occurring patterns of deployment within teams of different size.

4-member Teams				Frequency Ranking
R	=	20	instances (R2 = 16	
			(R3 = 4	
U	=	2		R
H	=	8		H
C	=	2		E
E	=	4		G
G	=	3		U
W	=	1		C
				W
		40		

3-member Teams				
R	=	15	instances (R2 = 11	
			(R3 = 3	
			(R1 = 1	
U	=	2		R
H	=	6		H
G	=	3		EG
E	=	3		U
W	=	1		W
		30		

2-member Teams				
R	=	11	instances (R2 = 7	
			(R3 = 3	
			(R1 = 1	
H	=	2		R
U	=	1		H & E
E	=	2		U)
S	=	1		S)
C	=	1		C)
W	=	1		W)
G	=	1		G)
		20		

1 member Working Alone				
S	=	3	instances	S
R	=	2	instances (R2 = 1	
			(R3 = 1	R
E	=	1		E)
H	=	1		H)
C	=	1		C)
W	=	1		W)
G	=	1		G)
		10		

Table 8: ARD:1 - Within most frequently occuring patterns of deployment the proportionate representation of activities associated with children and activities associated with nursery organization.

	Activities Assoc. with Children	Activities Assoc. with Nursery Org.	Total
4 member Teams	2	2	4
	3	1	4
	2	2	4
	3	1	4
	4	–	4
	2	2	4
	3	1	4
	2	2	4
	4	–	4
	3	1	4
	28 = 70%	12 = 30%	40
3 member Teams	3	–	3
	3	–	3
	2	1	3
	1	2	3
	2	1	3
	1	2	3
	2	1	3
	1	2	3
	3	–	3
	3	–	3
	21 = 70%	9 = 30%	30
2 member Teams	1	1	2
	2	–	2
	2	–	2
	1	1	2
	1	1	2
	2	–	2
	2	–	2
	2	–	2
	1	1	2
	2	–	2
	16 = 80%	4 = 20%	20
1 Member of Staff Working Alone	8 = 80%	2 = 20%	10

The derivation of role differentiation score

In response to questionnaire ARD:8 (Appendix (A)), head teachers or teachers-in-charge indicated how responsibility for various aspects of work in the nursery was divided between the various adults in the nursery.

The questionnaire covered six summary aspects of work: supervision, care and welfare of children; housework; administration; planning and organization of children's activities; supervision of and involvement in children's activities; contact with parents, visitors, students and other staff.

Each aspect was characterized by 10 examples of specific activities, and against each example the adults *mainly* responsible for it were indicated: this could be one or several, depending upon whether responsibility was exclusive to adults of one type or shared.

For each of the six summary aspects of nursery work, a count was made of the specific activities ascribed to teachers or assistants only. In some nurseries a number of the 60 items were neither teachers' responsibilities nor assistants'; for example in nursery classes some administrative and caretaking duties were undertaken by the primary school. In order to allow for this, teachers' and assistants' responsibility scores were standardized as illustrated in the following table:

Table 9

Summary Aspect	Teachers' or Assistants' Responsibility	Teachers' Responsibility	Assistants' Responsibility
Supervision	10	10	7
Housework	8	3	8
Administration	9	8	1
Planning	10	9	7
Involvement	10	10	9
Adult Contracts	10	10	2
TOTALS	57	50	34

STANDARDIZED PROPORTIONATE SCORES		
Teachers	$(50 \times 60 - 57)$ =	53
Nursery Assistants	$(34 \times 60 - 57)$ =	36
NURSERY'S ROLE DIFFERENTIATION SCORE	=	89

The proportionate scores of teachers and assistants when added together gave a figure that reflected, by its position on a high/low scale, the degree of role differentiation that existed in a nusery.

The differentiation scale varied between limits of 60 and 120: 60 would be the score in the extreme case where all 60 activities were the responsibility of either teachers or assistants but never of both; 120 would be the other extreme where responsibility for all 60 activities was shared equally between teachers and assistants.

A continuum from high to low role differentiation was constructed from scores obtained in this way, and nurseries were separated into four levels approximating to the quartiles on the actual distribution of scores.

Since several nurseries shared the same position on the scales, the actual allocation was as follows:

high	= 0 to 23rd percentile	:	9 nurseries
mod.high	= 27th to 53rd percentile	:	12 nurseries
mod.low	= 57th to 80th percentile	:	11 nurseries
low	= 82nd to 100th percentile	:	8 nurseries

Table 10

	SCORE	SCHOOLS	CLASS	SCH.	UNIT	NO. OF NURSERIES
			ROLE DIFFERENTIATION SCORES			
HIGH	81	075			1	1
	82					–
	83	027, 028	2			2
	84	006, 031	1	1		2
	85	030, 082		1	1	2
	86	036, 078	2			2
			5	2	2	9
MOD HIGH	87					–
	88	005, 080	1	1		2
	89	086, 091	1	1		2
	90	008, 096	2			2
	91	010, 035, 077	2		1	3
	92	017, 026, 095	3			3
			9	2	1	12
MOD LOW	93	051, 079	1	1		2
	94					–
	95	007, 085, 090	2	1		3
	96	025, 041, 066	2	1		3
	97	016, 046, 057	2		1	3
	98					–
	99					–
			7	3	1	11
LOW	100	040		1		1
	101	047, 056	2			2
	102					–
	103	015, 045	1		1	2
	104					–
	105	065,	1			1
	106					–
	107	042,		1		1
	108					–
	109	055	1			1
			5	2	1	8
		TOTALS	26	9	5	40

Table 11: Activity frequency: means and standard deviations: ARD:2

	Level of Role Diff:	High	Mod.High	Mod.Low	Low
Housework	Mean SD N	4.00000 5.96966 18	2.87500 3.13899 24	5.18182 5.13287 22	6.68750 6.90622 16
Equipment	Mean SD N	11.55556 5.78255 18	14.20833 6.42670 24	16.500000 6.66726 22	13.00000 8.52447 16
Administration	Mean SD N	2.61111 3.05130 18	8.75000 2.47158 24	3.59091 3.81300 22	3.68750 2.91476 16
Pass.Supv.	Mean SD N	2.22222 5.46169 18	1.62500 3.01896 24	4.22727 8.87979 22	2.31250 3.07069 16
Supervision	Mean SD N	56.88889 23.93837 18	59.29167 22.96212 24	50.63636 24.64712 22	47.12500 16.83201 16
Conversation	Mean SD N	15.38889 6.65219 18	17.91667 7.95595 24	17.77273 8.35482 22	16.62500 6.05392 16
Welfare	Mean SD N	12.94444 7.26371 18	16.16667 9.89803 24	9.86364 7.61762 22	11.87500 12.37134 16
Adult talk	Mean SD N	23.44444 11.87792 18	22.54167 8.23555 24	24.50000 11.80295 22	30.93750 14.41050 16
Involvement	Mean SD N	45.33333 16.56360 18	53.3333 18.77016 24	34.95455 15.97461 22	37.25000 18.92969 16

T
e
a
c
h
e
r
s

Housework	Mean SD N	15.22222 9.72901 18	10.25000 7.90844 24	9.13636 6.08116 22	14.37500 9.12780 16
Equipment	Mean SD N	21.33333 10.05280 18	17.58333 7.21060 24	18.50000 11.89538 22	22.43750 14.56465 16
Administration	Mean SD N	1.44444 2.20220 18	.54167 1.02062 24	.90909 2.59870 22	1.00000 1.59164 16
Pass.supv.	Mean SD N	2.66667 4.04388 18	3.04167 3.90628 24	2.45455 3.66096 22	1.25000 2.51661 16
Supervision	Mean SD N	48.27778 10.80188 18	47.41667 22.50588 24	49.63636 16.44774 22	49.31250 15.56800 16
Conversation	Mean SD N	15.27788 8.40032 18	15.70833 10.63415 24	14.90902 7.67128 22	16.18750 11.27959 16
Welfare	Mean SD N	17.22222 10.69665 18	16.45833 13.07829 24	16.59691 9.54019 22	10.56250 7.21081 16
Adult talk	Mean SD N	32.16667 21.37687 18	19.45833 9.66832 24	25.27275 12.23649 22	29.00000 10.03328 16
Involvement	Mean SD N	34.66667 15.80395 18	37.37500 16.42324 24	32.13636 14.88732 22	30.50000 14.84587 16

Assistants

Table 12: Activity frequency: MANOVA, ANOVA, analysis results

1. *Interaction: qualification (teacher; assistant) × role differentiation*

Multivariate Test of Significance

	Eigenvalue	Wilks Lambda	F	Hypothesis D	F	Error D	F	Signif. of F	Canon Corr.
1	.10773	.80652	1.19192	27.00000		421.19658		.23502	.31185
2	.06441	.89340	1.04724	16.00000		289.00000		.40667	.24599
3	.05159	.95094	1.06862	7.00000		145.00000		.38665	.22149

Univariate F-Tests all non-significant at the 5% level

2a. *Main effects: role differentiation*

	Eigenvalue	Wilks Lambda	F	Hypothesis D	F	Error D	F	Signif. of F	Canon Corr.
1	.21657	.76328	1.51170	27.00000		421.19658		.05017	.42192
2	.06084	.92859	.68168	16.00000		289.00000		.81174	.23948
3	.01514	.98508	.31371	7.00000		145.00000		.94687	.12214

Univariate F-Tests　　　　　　　　　　　　　r_{AC}

HOUSEWORK	P<.05	−.42762
ADULT TALK	P<.05	−.22316
INVOLVEMENT	P<.01	.58399

all others non significant at 5% level

2b. *Main effects: qualification* (teacher; assistant)

	Eigenvalue	Wilks Lambda	F	Hypothesis D	F	Error D	F	Signif. of F	Canon Corr.
1	.65504	.60422	10.48061	9.00000		144.00000		.00001	.62911

Univariate F-Tests　　　　　　　　　　　　　r_{AC}

HOUSEWORK	P<.00001	.67930
EQUIPMENT	P<.001	.39319
ADULT TALK	P<.00001	−.53889
INVOLVEMENT	P<.001	−.35546

r_{AC} is the correlation (r) between the activity (A) and the canonical composite of activities which best discriminates between the factors being compared (high/low role differentiation; qualification). The greater the magnitude of this correlation, the greater is the contribution of the particular activity to discriminating between the factors being compared: the contribution of each may thus be put in rank order according to the magnitude of r_{AC}.

Table 13: Activity duration: means and standard deviations: ARD:2

T e a c h e r s

Level of Role Diff:		High	Mod.High	Mod.Low	Low
Housework	Mean	178.1111	149.41667	272.36364	334.68750
	SD	257.6499	299.29670	352.98544	321.71058
	N	18	24	22	16
Equipment	Mean	613.83333	641.66667	948.18182	815.87500
	SD	503.03751	338.46837	532.99278	643.51927
	N	18	24	22	16
Administration	Mean	304.38889	166.79167	215.27273	230.18750
	SD	375.91710	200.74340	361.69932	284.61113
	N	18	24	22	16
Pass.Supv.	Mean	81.61111	71.54167	153.18133	60.12500
	SD	220.61682	159.17286	301.56159	82.54847
	N	18	24	22	16
Supervision	Mean	1856.33333	1884.33333	1837.13636	1365.06250
	SD	822.17185	643.45485	937.53061	713.05619
	N	18	24	22	16
Conversation	Mean	497.00000	663.62500	591.90909	612.68750
	SD	239.49113	293.99775	390.80538	300.47822
	N	18	24	22	16
Welfare	Mean	508.33333	627.04167	358.50000	528.81250
	SD	503.01000	424.98230	271.60489	565.30808
	N	18	24	22	16
Adult talk	Mean	738.94444	655.79167	861.13636	1102.37500
	SD	504.92905	284.86442	514.68060	859.71428
	N	18	24	22	16
Involvement	Mean	4221.44444	4140.12500	3764.18182	3943.62500
	SD	1196.28991	961.01076	1792.53586	1390.05248
	N	18	24	22	16

Assistants		Mean			
Housework	Mean	1247.33333	856.50000	549.27273	1077.12500
	SD	1006.75968	814.75566	421.14698	735.22939
	N	18	24	22	16
Equipment	Mean	1139.83333	859.41667	821.77273	1400.18750
	SD	541.71224	444.33056	600.63347	789.31043
	N	18	24	22	16
Administration	Mean	95.55556	41.83333	72.81818	24.50000
	SD	150.60748	94.42626	243.85312	52.72318
	N	18	24	22	16
Pass.supv.	Mean	272.38889	155.37500	104.22727	67.00000
	SD	504.42782	283.43588	160.21531	154.63549
	N	18	24	22	16
Supervision	Mean	1420.5000	1500.54167	1700.50000	1522.06250
	SD	588.81958	803.31032	851.00264	571.00814
	N	18	24	22	16
Conversation	Mean	526.05556	579.41667	592.31818	474.00000
	SD	498.41920	375.84293	517.20249	318.43869
	N	18	24	22	16
Welfare	Mean	702.38889	638.95833	705.54545	511.06250
	SD	518.91098	454.71828	519.12249	377.37116
	N	18	24	22	16
Adult talk	Mean	830.22222	598.37500	786.31818	818.06250
	SD	655.03413	492.02835	619.88366	308.33498
	N	18	24	22	16
Involvement	Mean	2766.05556	3770.00000	3709.68182	3106.13750
	SD	1295.35648	1247.11936	1762.36574	1062.91487
	N	18	24	22	16

Table 14: Activity duration: MANOVA, ANOVA, analysis results

1. *Interaction: qualification (teacher; assistant) × role differentiation*

Multivariate Test of Significance

	Eigenvalue	Wilks Lambda	F	Hypothesis	Error	Signif. of F	Canon Corr.
1	.18867	.77494	1.42317	27.00000	421.19658	.08027	.39840
2	.05958	.92114	.75731	16.00000	289.00000	.73325	.23713
3	.02457	.97602	.50887	7.00000	145.00000	.82676	.15485

Univariate F-Tests r_{AC}

HOUSEWORK $P<.05$ −.54365
EQUIPMENT $P<.05$ −.58733
all others non-significant at the 5% level.

2a. *Main effects: role differentiation*

	Eigenvalue	Wilks Lambda	F	Hypothesis	Error	Signif. of F	Canon Corr.
1	.15250	.78029	1.38307	27.00000	421.19658	.09833	.36376
2	.06408	.89929	.98460	16.00000	289.00000	.47358	.24540
3	.04503	.95691	.93276	7.00000	145.00000	.48320	.20758

Univariate F-Tests r_{AC}

EQUIPMENT $P<.05$ −.56333
all others non-significant at the 5% level.

2b. *Main effects: qualification (teacher, assistant)*

	Eigenvalue	Wilks Lambda	F	Hypothesis	Error	Signif. of F	Canon Corr.
1	.55565	.64282	8.89037	9.00000	144.00000	.00001	.89765

Univariate F-Tests r_{AC}

HOUSEWORK $P<.00001$ −.79934
EQUIPMENT $P<.01$ −.33406
ADMINISTRATION $P<.0001$ .46164
INVOLVEMENT $P<.01$ .31019

All others non-significant at the 5% level